Tara emanates joy, authenticity, and a genuine interest in others, and she's somehow managed to put all of that into *Eat. Pie. Love.* This book is an earnest call to gather together with Jesus at the center and to learn from him. Her recipes are the icing on the cake . . . or I should say pie!

—Marjie Schaefer, Flourish Through the Word Ministries,
Seattle, Washington

An eloquent and honest account of a lifelong commitment and passion. It transcends courage and conviction and becomes an inspiration.

—Celeste Shaw, owner of Chaps Bakery, Seattle, Washington,
and editor of *Flea Market Style Magazine* and *Where Women Create*

Tara Royer brings the truth, the food, and Jesus in abundance in *Eat. Pie. Love.* Each page of this book is an invitation to sit across the table from a good friend and talk about the hard things, the brave things, and the God things. And laugh! Trust me, you're going to want to savor every bite!

—Kathleen Y'Barbo, bestselling author of *The Pirate Bride*
and the *Secret Lives of Will Tucker* series

Tara is honest, brave, and the very definition of a warrior. She makes the world around her brighter and better and reflects Jesus in all that she does. *Eat. Pie. Love.* embodies everything I love about Tara, and it's my new go-to gift for everyone in my life!

—Melanie Shankle, bestselling author and speaker

When I see a book filled with Scripture, encouragement, sweet art, and pie, that is a recipe for delight. Tara is not only your go-to gal for her amazing baking skills, but she will also become your fast friend and lead you into sweet time with the Lord. *Eat. Pie. Love.* is a jewel of a devotional.

—Sarah Martin, speaker and author of *Just RISE UP!*

Tara's biblical reminders, whimsical illustrations, and delicious recipes are just the thing to bring comfort and encouragement to both body and soul. This book will bring joy to the people you love and makes a perfect gift.

—Susie Davis, author, speaker,
and cofounder of Austin Christian Fellowship

In a world starving for real, Tara Royer Steele's words in *Eat. Pie. Love.* nourish us. The pages of this book left me full and grateful.

—Lisa Whittle, author, founder of Ministry Strong,
podcast host of *Jesus Over Everything*

Tara has creatively taken all the pain and lessons of her past and woven them into daily inspirational bites for us to chew on. Her love for Jesus and others graciously drips from these pages.

—Cheryl Moses, writer and coach

In *Eat. Pie. Love.*, Tara gives comfort, combats lies with the truth of Scripture, and shares wisdom from her own life.

—Angie Gillikin, author

A delicious bite of reality mixed with purposeful encouragement that offers a balance of sweet moments and salty sass! Top it all off with mouthwatering tried and true recipes, and you have yourself *Eat. Pie. Love.*

—Stephanie Gilbert, anchor for KXAN, Austin, Texas

Tara reminds us in *Eat. Pie. Love.* that it's in the flaky places of our lives where God meets us and reminds us that love is stronger, deeper, and fuller than we dared to imagine. May you find yourself rolling out the dough of your life.

—KariAnn Lessner, podcast host of *You Brew You*

We all go through seasons when we need God's Word spoon-fed to us in devotional form, and I cannot imagine a better way to have that served up than with *Eat. Pie. Love.* Each day, you will be filled with God's Word, encouraged by Tara's thoughts, and challenged in the daily "Slice of Pie." This book is worth grabbing for the recipes alone!

—Becky Kiser, speaker and author of *Sacred Holidays* and *More Jesus*

Inside the pages of *Eat. Pie. Love.*, Tara Royer Steele speaks with humor, relatable truth, and an extra measure of bravery and invites you into a conversation overflowing with grace—the kind of grace that changes you from the inside out and overflows into every part of your life.

—Meredith King, author and executive director of Integrus Leadership

Tara's recipes should be the types that are kept secret and only passed from generation to generation, but in her typical spirit of hospitality, she shares them with us in this beautiful book of devotional thoughts, unique artwork, and scrumptious treats. Give yourself or someone you love a blessing with *Eat. Pie. Love.* You'll treasure it for years to come.

—Patty H. Scott, author of *Slow Down, Mama*

I first enjoyed a taste of Tara Royer Steele's *Eat. Pie. Love.* on the very same day that I tasted her lemon berry pie. Psalm 34:8 immediately came to mind: taste and see that the Lord is good. *Eat. Pie. Love.* challenges, encourages, blesses, and never fails to whet your appetite for more God. And more pie.

—Dana Knox Wright, author and blogger

Like Tara, this recipe for life doesn't beat around the bush. She tells it like it is, and it is just what you need to hear: heart, soul, and the gritty truth all wrapped up in a pretty lattice-style crust.

—Jolie Sikes Smith, Junk Gypsy, Round Top, Texas

This book is a treasure, and you'll find yourself reaching for her words again and again. And even if you don't cook, you'll drool over her recipes!

—Melody Ross, artist, author, speaker, teacher, and coach

Eat. Pie. Love. is a great resource for those who love good food and want to grow in their understanding of God's grace and their identity in the gospel.

—Kyle Ogle, pastor, Center Church, Brenham, Texas

What a fun way to engage Scripture! Tara's combination of personal testimony, recipes, artwork, and thoughtful questions invite you to experience God with all of your senses!

—Debbie Byrd, worship leader
and author of *God's Word In My Heart At Bedtime*

Tara Royer Steele combines art, Scripture, stories, and delicious recipes that feed your soul! You'll walk away with hope, love, transformation, and the secret to Junkberry Pie, my family's favorite.

—Paige Hull, blogger and owner of The Vintage Round Top

From her words to her art and all of her tried and true family recipes, you will be encouraged to love Jesus and people better as Tara shares little slices of her own life journey in *Eat. Pie. Love.*

—Stephanie Holden, speaker, artist, and influencer,
Brigg's Chapel, Porterville, Missouri

Tara has opened the café doors to her heart in *Eat. Pie. Love.* not only for us to experience the sweetness of her soul and delicious pies but also to taste and see that the Lord is good!

—Ruthie Winans, Sugar Pie Farmhouse

Eat. Pie. Love. is comfort food for the body and soul. In its pages, Tara celebrates the fact that life is sometimes like her junkberry pie: messy and random but worth it in the end.

—Lincee Ray, author of *Why I Hate Green Beans* and *It's A Love Story*

Tara brings love and grace to the table, and now you can bring those same qualities into your home with *Eat. Pie. Love.*— complete with Tara's recipes, famous hand lettering, and artwork to help bind the Scriptures and messages to your heart.

—Jolie Gray, founder of Purpose Box

In *Eat. Pie. Love.,* Tara shares with her honest and vulnerable heart how the Lord meets us right where we are. This book will remind you that we are all connected to one another, and sometimes something as simple as pie is enough to gather us.

—Jeanne Oliver, artist

Created straight from her heart, Tara's encouraging writing, unique drawings, and made-with-love recipes make *Eat. Pie. Love.* a book that folks will grab time and time again! I cannot wait for y'all to meet my beautiful friend and Texas-treasure, Tara Royer Steele!

—Jeane Wynn, Wynn Wynn Media

Eat.
Pie.
Love.

52 Devotions to Satisfy Your Mind, Body, and Soul

Tara Royer Steele

BroadStreet
PUBLISHING

BroadStreet Publishing® Group, LLC
Savage, Minnesota, USA
BroadStreetPublishing.com

Eat. Pie. Love. : 52 Devotions to Satisfy Your Mind, Body, and Soul

978-1-4245-5946-6 (hardcover)
978-1-4245-5947-3 (e-book)

Stock or custom editions of BroadStreet Publishing titles may be purchased in bulk for educational, business, ministry, fundraising, or sales promotional use. For information, please email info@broadstreetpublishing.com.

The author is represented by Alive Literary Agency, 7680 Goddard Street, Suite 200, Colorado Springs, Colorado, 80920, www.aliveliterary.com.

Cover and interior by Garborg Design at GarborgDesign.com

Printed in China
20 21 22 23 24 5 4 3 2 1

To the grace gang.

Y'all know how to pour the best ingredients

into my life. Y'all are my favorite slice of pie.

Of course, topped with vanilla ice cream.

Contents

Foreword

By Melanie Shankle

I first met Tara in the middle of her family's famous restaurant, Royers Round Top Café, in Round Top, Texas. It was packed and overflowing as it always is during Spring Antique Week, yet she had graciously reserved a last-minute spot at a table for my friends and me. We should have made arrangements months ago, but we hadn't even thought to! This was my first time dining at Royers, and it only took one bite of my meal to understand why their reservation book fills up weeks in advance.

The thing that stood out to me more than the dinner and the pies (oh, the pies. Yes, that's plural. Don't judge me. I could write love songs about the pies.) was the graciousness and hospitality of our hostess for the evening. Tara wrapped me up in one of her hugs like we were old friends instead of new acquaintances. And I watched as she made everyone else in her path feel the same way that evening. I knew immediately that she was the real deal.

A few months later, I was talking to my publisher about where I could film the video portion of my Bible study, *Church of the Small Things*, and I knew just the place. With some hesitation, I emailed Tara and asked if we could use Royers for a recording session. It felt like a big ask because I know how busy they are and how much they have going on at all times. I can't tell you how thrilled I was when she said Royers would be happy to oblige because here's the thing: *Church of the Small Things* is about letting God use you exactly where you are to do all of the day-to-day things that might seem insignificant but are actually making a big difference in the lives around you. I couldn't think of anyone who lives that out more than Tara.

Tara has bloomed right where God has planted her in spite of struggles, obstacles, and often roughness of her path. The longer I live, the more I watch to see how someone truly lives as rather than simply listen to the words they say. Talk is cheap in this world of social media and clever Instagram captions. As I got to know Tara, I quickly learned that she lives every bit of what she proclaims to believe. She serves her family and the world around her. She invests in her community and finds ways to make it better. She loves with her whole heart, and if she tells you she's praying for you, then she absolutely means it. She talks about being brave and then actually takes huge leaps of faith to try something new. She's not afraid to dig right into the messiest parts of life to find healing and wholeness.

And I'm not saying she's perfect. She'd be the first to tell you she's not, which is one of the many reasons I find her so endearing. She bares her heart, soul, and all of her flaws. She isn't afraid to share the not-so-pretty parts of her story. I am not one for small talk, and I appreciate a person who isn't afraid to dive right in. That's Tara. She dives right in to all the joy, pain, growth, and challenges that life has to offer and trusts God to guide her steps when the way doesn't seem clear.

The bottom line is I love Tara Royer Steele. She's real, she's funny, she's bold, and she can make a pie so good that you'll decide your new diet is a pie for every meal and a prayer for a miracle for your cholesterol and blood sugar. As you read the pages of this book, I have no doubt you will fall in love with her heart, her cooking, and her passion to follow God wherever he leads.

Melanie Shankle

New York Times bestselling author and speaker

Introduction

Hey, friend! I am so glad you are here! Sit down and make yourself comfortable. Grab a big ole cup of coffee and your favorite blanket and get cozy.

I wrote this book picturing God sitting right next to me, asking him which parts of my story, which hard-learned lessons, which victories and joys he wanted me to share. He answered me with pictures and with words, each of which I've done my best to put on paper to share with y'all. I'm also sharing with you some of my favorite recipes that I've gathered along this journey; some I've created when I just needed some quiet time with God, and some I've made with friends and family during celebrations. Together, the words and the recipes create a story of grace, hope, and love. My prayer for every one of you is that you'll find a quiet space and see that you are worth this time of leaning in to him. Let God lead you through these pages just like he led me.

But before we get started, I just want to remind you of a few things:

You are loved.

You are seen.

You are worthy.

You are meant to be here, holding this book in your hands.

You have a story that needs to be told.

Are you ready? Alright, let's dig in.

1

Divine Circles

I am doing a new thing! Now it springs up;
do you not perceive it? I am making a way in the
wilderness and streams in the wasteland.

Isaiah 43:19

When I look at some of the most unexpected
blessings in my life, I can trace them back to a divine
appointment that led to another encounter and then
another. As I remember each of the events and people
that led to each blessing, I see a divine circle start to
form—a circle that all started with one encounter but
brought me to a beautiful blessing in the end. If you
think about it, I'm sure you have examples of your own

divine circles. God uses so many things and people in our lives to bless us beyond our expectations.

Let me give you a little history about one of God's divine circles in my life. It was during the time of the Texas Antiques Festival in Round Top, Texas—a three-week period when our town of ninety people turns into a town of one hundred thousand! We were in the throes of baking thousands of pies and cooking hundreds of pounds of chicken, and I was exhausted. An Instagram friend reached out to me and said she was coming in with a group of girlfriends she wanted me to meet. At the last minute, my friend couldn't make the trip, but the rest of the gang came along.

There were twelve of them, all beautiful ladies dressed in their best Round Top junkin' attire with lots of jewels, big Texas hair, and cowboy boots. I can still see them in my mind. They sat at one of only eleven tables in our cozy little café. I escaped the heat of the kitchen for just a moment, smelling of grease and pie, and approached the table with joy. Those girls were exactly what I needed right then. They breathed life into my weary soul. We visited, took pictures, and then they each gave me a card with a truth affirmation and encouragement on it. I stuck the cards into my pocket, and they went on their way.

A couple of years later, my husband and I were in the middle of transitioning out of our family business: Royers Round Top Café. We were selling the café to my brother and sister-in-law. Selling this business was certainly bittersweet! I had been working at that café for thirty years, and I was tired and weary, not sure what the heck the Lord had planned next for us. During that season, a woman named Melody Ross sent me a message on Facebook. When I saw her face, I recognized her as one of the twelve women from the antiques festival years before. She said, "I have a space at Brave Girl Camp in June, and I'd like for you to come." Of course, I immediately said I couldn't go because I was living in the lies that we couldn't afford it, I couldn't leave work, and my husband and kiddos couldn't handle life without me. I made up all the excuses I could. Well, guess what? My husband told me that I should make plans to go, saying he thought it was actually perfect timing. I broke down in tears.

When the time came for me to go to this Brave Girl Camp in Idaho, I was excited about the unknown. I couldn't wait to sit with a group of women I'd never met, drink coffee in my pj's, and rest. Ha-ha! God is so, so funny. What I didn't know was I had signed up for a soul restoration camp—a deep inner healing class that would help me work through my past and restore my beautiful soul. I immediately knew that God was doing something new in me. He had a plan, and that "chance" meeting orchestrated years earlier had led to something bigger and better that he had planned for me.

▲ Is there a divine appointment that has shifted and shaped your life for your good and for God's glory?

▲ Take a blank sheet of paper and draw a circle. Inside the circle, write a divine appointment that you have experienced (it could be a random meeting at a grocery store, in a restaurant, or over coffee). Then, from that circle, draw smaller circles and fill them with the blessings that have come out of that divine encounter.

2

How You Hold Your Words

The soothing tongue is a tree of life,
but a perverse tongue crushes the spirit.

PROVERBS 15:4

My words can flow so quickly at times and without a
filter. Often, without thinking about who I really am or
who I'm currently standing in front of (and also without
thinking about how God hears all my words), I just say
what's on my mind with little hesitation! I might not
cuss like a sailor, but at times, I can get pretty close.
Does that make me look cool or more like a fool? And
it's not only about foul language. How many times
have I said negative or hurtful things about someone
else? If I'm to be a light for Jesus, how do these ugly

words flying out of my mouth reflect him? We were created in God's image, and I'm pretty sure that he wouldn't drop expletives in casual conversation or say ugly things about others when frustrated with them. This is something that I'm seriously working on. I want to let the words that flow out from my mouth be a beautiful living example of him.

Okay, now let's switch gears to our thoughts. Yikes! I am pretty sure the words that sometimes swirl around in my head can be much worse than the ones that actually come out of my mouth, especially if I'm thinking of those thoughts in fear, bitterness, or in the middle of a disagreement that I'm not "winning." For many years, I thought the words that were spoken in my head didn't matter because as long as I didn't speak them out loud, no one heard them; therefore, no one was hurt, right? Um, nope. That's not true at all. Because God hears them. And not only does God hear them, but they are also like poison eating away at me. What was I thinking? My words—whether spoken aloud or in my head—matter!

Proverbs says "a perverse tongue crushes the spirit." *Perverse*. That word is harsh, and it's certainly not a word that I want my heavenly Father to associate with me. If we could hold the words of our hearts, minds, and souls in our hands, would we feel comfortable giving them to our heavenly Father? For me, I couldn't say that's true all the time. This is a real struggle in my life! It's not easy. But I have to ask myself: how will using these ugly words help fix anything? They won't. But God can help. So, the next time those words come swinging in like a wrecking ball, I know I can breathe deep, go to him first, and allow him to give me words. And you can too. I want the words that I speak and think to be words of hope, peace, and comfort. I want them to point people to Jesus.

Today's Slice of the Pie

▲ Are the words that flow from your mouth always spoken in gratitude and truth? Can you think of a time in the past week when that hasn't been the case?

▲ Today, how can the words you speak and think be like a tree of life to yourself and others? Would visualizing Jesus standing among your circle of friends help you?

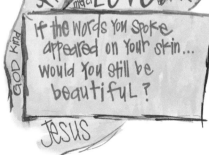

3

Love 'Em All

Let the message of Christ dwell among you richly as you teach and admonish one another with all wisdom through psalms, hymns, and songs from the Spirit, singing to God with gratitude in your hearts.

COLOSSIANS 3:16

It took me a long time to recognize that the people God had placed in my life were not judging me; they were holding me accountable. They were bright lights that could share from their experiences and add light to my darkness. God calls us to love people exactly where they are on their journey, even if we don't agree with them. That friend might be walking down the wrong path, but it's not our job to judge them.

So, what does holding someone accountable look like? It's simple: just show up and let God use you. You can sit next to them in silence, pray over them from a distance, speak truth over their lives, and help them embrace things from a different perspective. Then, just maybe they can get to a place where they own their mistakes, forgive themselves, and ask for forgiveness if needed. I believe the hardest part about holding the broken accountable is they usually respond with a reaction and emotions. Restored hearts know they can sit with the broken, and they don't need to react.

I want to surround myself with people who pick me up when I stumble or gently say, "Hey, does that feel like self-respect?" I want to be surrounded with friends who remind me of the joy right in front of me, not just the bad. I want to be the friend that can speak of God's promises and presence through the pain.

Today's Slice of the Pie

- ▲ Read Colossians 3:16 and ask the Lord to show you the joy in your life where you see nothing.

- ▲ Reflect back on a conversation where you felt judged. Ask the Lord to show you if there is something that you need to take from that conversation and grow from. If something comes to mind, write it down.

Royers Round Top Cafe
Original Pie Crust

Yield: 3 1-pound dough balls

INGREDIENTS

¼ tsp salt
1 cup water
5 cups white flour
2 cups Crisco shortening

INSTRUCTIONS

Dissolve the salt in the water and set aside.

Cut the Crisco into the flour with a fork or pastry cutter. When the mixture is crumbly, add the salt water and knead until the water is absorbed.

Add several tablespoons of flour and continue to knead the dough until it pulls cleanly away from your hands. Roll the dough into three separate balls and place each of them in a plastic bag and freeze until you are ready to use them.

When you are ready to use the dough, set it out to thaw for 3 to 4 hours or place in your refrigerator to thaw overnight.

The dough rolls out easiest at room temperature.

4

Position Yourself in the Silence

Do not be afraid; do not be discouraged.
Go out to face them tomorrow,
and the Lord will be with you.

2 Chronicles 20:17

I don't usually let all the moving parts of my ten-year-old son's baseball games get to me, but on one particular day, the emotions could not be stopped. I saw the frustration and pain on my son's face from the pitcher's mound, and I took it on too. I sat with him in his pain from the bleachers. He was having an off day and wasn't at his best, and I know he felt like he was letting his teammates down. I began to let what I thought others were saying about my son's performance get in my head. I started to believe that their kids could do better. Then, as I sat there in tears, I decided to pull myself together and not let others' opinions of my son affect my emotions. I wasn't going to let the stories I was making up ruin our last day of baseball for the season.

Through my tears, I began to see Jesus on the mound with Brayden. He was encouraging and loving him through his imperfections and teaching him about the lessons of baseball and life. He was sharing that it's not all about throwing strikes and making your team look good. The mistakes and the failures are important too because that's when you see what really makes a team. Baseball is about picking each other up when we strike out or miss a fly ball and learning to love our teammates through errors. Baseball is also a beautiful reminder that we need teammates—whether out there on the field or in life—because when we stand alone, the devil begins to creep in and speak lies over us. Just like in life, we need to position friends around us for when we strike out and the enemy starts to whisper lies in our ears.

Today's Slice of the Pie

▲ On the playing field, do you have your glove up and positioned to catch the enemy's curve balls at all times? In what areas of your life do you feel you're striking out?

▲ Who are the people in your life that you've positioned to speak truth when the enemy is speaking lies?

5

Peacekeeper vs. Peacemaker

An unfriendly person pursues selfish ends
and against all sound judgment starts quarrels.

PROVERBS 18:1

Have you ever thought of the difference between
being a peacemaker and a peacekeeper? I didn't think
much about it either—not for a long time. I thought
to be the peacekeeper was a good thing, but in the
last few years, I realized all it did was bring strife and
unrest. A peacekeeper goes around giving everyone
what they want to make them happy in the moment.

Well, there's a big problem in that: we can't give everyone what they want all the time. That doesn't solve a single thing. It only continues to enable people, showing them that they will be rewarded over and over no matter their behavior. Then, they continue to create more chaos, knowing that they will be lavished with more of what they want.

I tried to keep the peace for years in our family. Growing up and then running a family business puts you in the middle of not just the business but also the family. The family came to me with all their questions, wants, needs, and dreams. Goodness, the pressure to make everyone happy and give them what they wanted was unbearable at times and pushed me to provide them with all that they wanted for the moment. I did everything I could to avoid the issue.

Things would be good for a month, and then we were back where we started. Nothing was ever resolved; I just covered it up with a Band-Aid and hoped it would heal on its own. The wound wouldn't heal, though. It only got deeper and led to more conflict and strife, making me the bad guy. I was not a good friend or leader. And the peacekeeping was causing a huge rift in my marriage. I was choosing to keep my family happy over listening to my husband, who was leading. He wanted to help me, but I was deep in the ocean, relying on myself—and nearly drowning. I was tossing and turning and not once did I call out to Jesus for help. I believed I had what it took to stay afloat in the sea of requests.

Then, by the grace of God, I went to an event where I learned the difference between peacekeeping and peacemaking. My life shifted after that, and I took my power back. I could do this. In fact, I was created for this! I didn't have to just agree and appease. Instead, I learned I could step into hard places, embrace the situation, stop avoiding the conflict, and start speaking truth in love to shift the situation and create change. I had to be brave and do the hard things, but in the end, I knew God's truth would win. I realized that I had to bring a healing salve of truth to bring true peace. The result was a deeper intimacy with God and a healthier relationship with my family. It's not perfect because none of us is perfect. He might not always change their hearts, but he always changes mine. We must die to self and humble ourselves before him. Then he can open us up to receive the gift of healing and restoration.

Today's Slice of the Pie

▲ Do you think you are a peacekeeper or a peacemaker? Explain why.

▲ If you are a peacekeeper, how can you reevaluate a relationship and make peace instead of just keeping peace?

6

one

If a man has a hundred sheep and one of them
wanders away, what will he do? Won't he leave the
ninety-nine others on the hills and go out to search
for the one that is lost? And if he finds it, I tell you the
truth, he will rejoice over it more than over the ninety-
nine that didn't wander away! In the same way,
it is not my heavenly Father's will that even one
of these little ones should perish.

I've struggled with numbers for many years. Being in
the event and restaurant business, numbers matter.
*How many people came to your conference? How
many steaks did you cook tonight? How many pies*

did you sell? How many people did you cater to? How much money did you make tonight waiting tables? I would get lost in the numbers and think that if I didn't have 150 people at a conference, it wasn't enough. We weren't able to raise enough money to cover the costs or donate enough to a cause. Getting caught up in the numbers stole all my joy. I missed out on so many things because I was focusing on the one thing that was consuming me. No single thought should consume us other than Jesus. It is always about him, the one, and what he will do for one, even if the one is me. He sees each of us and cares for us individually instead of only as a large group that he is shepherding.

I was once at a retreat with another leader, and we talked about how we both thrived on numbers. We wondered why we got it in our heads that we had to have fifteen people at our weekend events. Where did that lie start? As soon as we were able to see this as a lie instead of the truth, we were able to focus on the one girl that needed to sit with other sisters going through the same thing. Then, I was able to apply that to the café—like when a state trooper came to eat on a slow night and told us that he had just delivered news to a mother that her son passed away in a car accident. God slowed our work down that night so that we could sit with him and hear his story. Sometimes God wants us to throw the numbers out the window and focus on just one. Because the truth is, Jesus cares about the one. He has shown us what he will do for just one.

Sometimes that one is a struggling girl or a heartbroken state trooper, and sometimes the one is me.

Today's Slice of the Pie

▲ Do you get caught up in numbers? If so, what area of your life do you let numbers consume you?

▲ If you took numbers out of the picture, how would your life look different?

▲ Is there one that you need to sit with and encourage? How can you do that today?

"if a man has a hundred sheep and ONE of them wanders away, what will he do? won't he leave the ninety-nine on the hills and go out to search for the ONE that is lost? and if he finds it, I tell you the truth, he will rejoice over it more than over the ninety-nine that didn't wander away! In the same way, it is not my heavenly Father's will that even ONE of these little ONE's should perish."

matt 18:12-14

1

Recipe for a Grit Girl

My dear brothers and sisters,
be strong and immovable.
Always work enthusiastically for the Lord,
for you know that nothing you do
for the Lord is ever useless.

1 CORINTHIANS 15:58 NLT

Being a follower of Christ takes grit. Having grit
requires us to follow our calling, use our God-given
gifts to persevere no matter what punches life throws
at us, and keep our faith deeply rooted and steady
through the storms.

Here's a recipe for a grit girl:

A pinch of determination
A dash of perseverance
A sprinkle of courage
A spoonful of curiosity
A drizzle of forgiveness
A dollop of integrity
A heaping scoop of grace

INSTRUCTIONS

Pull on a pair of well-worn boots, toss the above ingredients together, dig your hands in, and mix well.

Add a little bit more of each ingredient as needed, and you've got a well-seasoned grit girl standing in her truth.

TODAY'S SLICE OF THE PIE

▲ Your turn! If your life isn't exactly what you want it to be, write a recipe for the girl you know that you were created to be!

▲ What ingredients are you missing in your life? Are those keeping you from becoming a grit girl?

The Great Steak

Yield: 1 steak

Ingredients

10-ounce center-cut filet (or any size you want)
¼ cup lemon pepper
¼ cup coarse ground black pepper
¼ cup garlic powder
Dill butter (recipe below)

Instructions

Combine the spices in a bowl, then toss and coat each side of the filet in the spices.

Sear each side of the steak on an iron skillet set to 350° to 400°F until the seasoning becomes a crust, about 3 to 4 minutes on each side.

Cook until you reach the desired temperature, brushing with dill butter after each turn.

Dill Butter Recipe

Yield: 2 cups

Ingredients

1 cube chicken bouillon
1 tablespoon hot water
1 pound butter, softened
2 teaspoons dill flakes
1 teaspoon chopped garlic
¼ cup minced onion

Instructions

Place the chicken bouillon cube in a microwavable container with one tablespoon of water and heat for one minute. Stir until dissolved.

Combine the chicken bouillon mixture, softened butter, and remaining ingredients in a bowl.

Store in an air-tight container in the refrigerator.

This sauce is great on most anything—except maybe ice cream!

8

Be the Hands and Feet of Jesus

How are they to preach unless they are sent?
As it is written, "How beautiful are the feet of those
who preach the good news!"

ROMANS 10:15 ESV

I grew up waiting tables in our family business, starting
when I was twelve years old. And let me tell you,
waiting on tables will humble you really quick. The
snap of a finger to fill water glasses and I came running
with a smile. Okay, most of the time. I'm thankful for
the grace extended to me that taught me to extend
grace to others. I have been told that I give grace too

be the hands & feet of JESUS

often. Man, wouldn't it stink if Jesus said, "Oh, I'm sorry. I've given you your fair share of grace. Now you're on your own"? Phew! Praise the Lord that's not the case.

The guests that walked through our café doors were often looking for an escape from the city, to get away from the hard stuff. They came to rest, to be loved on, and filled up. It was our job to meet their needs. What a gift, right? We had no idea what chapter of their story they were walking, but we needed to be a light in the middle of it—to speak kindness, to love, and to give them a big ole Jesus smile. It's not easy being the hands and feet of Jesus, but he is in us and will sustain us when we are tired and weary and through it. And, in return, we will be filled with treasures all day long.

Today's Slice of the Pie

▲ Where are some places you go on a routine basis that you can be the hands and feet of Jesus? The checkout lines? The school car line?

▲ What do you think it means to be truly covered in grace?

▲ How can you extend grace to someone that you see on a regular basis?

▲ Where can you carve out time to sit with Jesus and let him show you what grace—love, forgiveness, peace, and hope—looks like?

9

Harsh vs. Gentle Teacher

Gracious words are a honeycomb,
sweet to the soul and healing to the bones.

PROVERBS 16:24

We all have our favorite teacher from school, or most
of us do! Of course, my favorite teachers were my
favorite because they weren't too hard on me and
loved me for me! But sometimes in our lives, we need
a gentle teacher *and* a harsh teacher. Have you ever
had a friend who can at times be a harsh teacher?
When they are honest, do you see them as rude and
not want to be their friend anymore? When we can
work through our damaged narrative, we can take their

words and see that they want God's best for us. Their words can be gracious and full of truth.

I have had a few harsh teachers in my life, but my favorite one is my husband, Rick. Yes, I know that seems hard to believe, but he sees me and knows me. He knows when to push me and remind me that I'm better than being a doormat, allowing people to walk all over me. My favorite memory of this fills me with hope when I think about it, but it sure didn't feel like it in the moment! One day we were driving down the back roads to Round Top, and he looked so strong and protective. He spoke with passion over a tough relationship I was letting stand between us. He asked how we even got to this place in our marriage and how we were even still married. "We can't keep going like this," he started. "You are going to have to trust me and know that I only want what is best for you, for us, and for our family. I love you."

My heart fell into my stomach and tears started to pour down my face. Was he truly thinking of divorce? Of course, I knew he wasn't because we have so much grace for each other, but we were at the end of the rope. I was going to have to let go and trust that I would land on solid ground. Then, my phone rang, and it was the person I was letting stand between Rick and me. I didn't want to answer it; I tried to ignore it, hoping everything would fix itself. But I dug down deep and answered the phone. Of course, they began asking the very questions I didn't want them to ask, questions where they needed and wanted things I

gracious words are like a honeycomb, sweetness to the soul & health to the body.
Proverbs 16:24

couldn't give. But because of the conversation I had just had with Rick, I knew I had to trust him and Jesus. And Jesus was near! He helped me stand in truth and speak the hard words I needed to say. The person didn't respond in the way I expected. Instead, they said, "I understand."

Without Rick's harsh yet loving challenge to me, I know I wouldn't have had the courage to stand up for myself and my marriage. Having someone in our corner who is willing to say the hard things we need to hear forces us to take a good look at ourselves, and it helps us to grow. Harsh but gentle teachers can be a gift from God. We just have to humble ourselves enough to listen because God may just be using them to speak to us.

TODAY'S SLICE OF THE PIE

- ▲ Can you think of a conversation where you thought someone was being too critical or rude to you? If you could look at that conversation from a different perspective, what do you think you can learn from their words?

- ▲ Do you see yourself as a harsh or gentle teacher? Why?

- ▲ Think about a time that God was a harsh and gentle teacher. What was he trying to teach you?

10

Knocked Upside the Head

Each of you must put off falsehood
and speak truthfully to your neighbor,
for we are all members of one body.

EPHESIANS 4:25

There have been many times in my life when I've finally had that "aha" moment. You know, that moment when God keeps speaking and you finally catch on. I'd like to share five of those "aha" moments with you. Maybe they will speak to you too.

1. "We don't need to change. We need to get back to who we were originally created to be by the Father." I thought I had to change who I was, but what I needed to do was change my learned

47

behaviors. To do that I needed to dig deep and see where those behaviors started and work through the layers.

2. "They are doing the best they could with the knowledge, truth, love, and hope they had." I guess I just figured my parents had it all figured out, right? That they read the book that told them how to parent perfectly. Well, nope! Once I was knocked upside the head with the truth that my parents do the best they can, it was so much easier for me to extend grace and mercy.

3. "They might never change." This one is hard to process, but it's the truth. Sadly, that person you wish would change might not be able to. They may never get unstuck. Still, you can keep being a light for them.

4. "Is your narrative damaged or positive?" Oh my goodness! I spoke a damaged narrative for most of my life. When we can step back and see that we do have a voice, that we are powerful, that we do have a choice, and that we don't need to be a victim, we can take our life back.

5. "We are called to love people until it brings us to tears and breaks our hearts." Ouch. We are called to love people in the beginning, the middle, and the end of their story. We might not be there for all the parts, but from my experience, I know that through the breaking of others, you will be broken, and it will draw you closer to God.

Today's Slice of the Pie

▲ What are some "aha" moments that either God or others have spoken to you that knocked you upside the head, stuck with you, and helped you walk home?

▲ What lies are you holding on to that are keeping you stuck? What truths can you speak in place of those lies?

Tara's Jalapeno Cheese Grits

Yield: Feeds 12 to 15

INGREDIENTS

4½ cups water
¼ cup diced jalapeños, canned or pickled
¼ cup chopped garlic • ½ teaspoon paprika
½ teaspoon cayenne • ¼ pound butter
1 tablespoon salt • 12 ounces grits • 2 eggs
¾ pound Pepper Jack cheese slices
1 pound American cheese slices
4 ounces cream cheese • 2 cups water
2 cups heavy whipping cream

INSTRUCTIONS

Bring 4½ cups of water to boil in a large pot. Add the jalapeños, garlic, paprika, cayenne, butter, and salt. Stir until the butter is melted.

Pour the grits into the hot water and stir. Turn off the heat and cover for 5 minutes.

Add the eggs and stir until combined. Add the Pepper Jack, American, and cream cheese. Stir until nearly melted.

Add in 2 cups of water and 2 cups heavy whipping cream. Turn to low heat and stir constantly until heated through.

11

Christ's Family Quilt

My God will meet all your needs according to the riches of his glory in Christ Jesus.

PHILIPPIANS 4:19

I'm often asked: how do you find your tribe? I have had many tribes in my life, and for nearly forty years I truly believed that certain people in my life were the ones—the ones that would come running no matter what, the ones that would be in my tribe forever. Sadly, that wasn't true. For a season of my life, I was the one buying all the drinks at the party, the fun one, so who wouldn't want to jump into my car? I was buying! If I had been honest with myself in that season, I would have admitted that I just wanted someone to love me and to feel needed. I wasn't living my best life and being who God created me to be. Those weren't my people; they weren't pouring truth, hope, or peace into my life either. All they did was take.

It takes many years and lots of hard work to find a true tribe, people who will stand by you through the sanctification of your life. Until recently, I honestly didn't understand that some people are only meant to be in our lives for a season. Early in my faith, I thought friends left because I did something wrong. But, looking back, I understand that God had them there for a season. They were there to help me learn something. Sometimes it takes digging deep into our faith, but eventually we can ask the question, "God, what did you want me to learn from that relationship?" Maybe they provided warmth and peace during a hard time in your life. Perhaps they were there to show you what joy felt like again. Maybe they hurt you, and through the pain, it taught you about forgiveness and letting go. Regardless of the reason, they will forever be etched into your heart.

Are you still stuck on that friend who left or that situation you don't yet understand? Open up your hands and let the light in. Ask God what you were supposed to learn from it. Today, as I run this race with him, he brings people to encourage, speak the truth, and run beside me. Let him bring your tribe to you. They might not look like what you wanted, and they may not be who you thought they should be, but they are precisely what you need. The family of Christ is like

a big, comfy, worn, and tattered quilt. At times all we can do is drag it along with us, but the good news is that it's strong enough and can take the beating. Other times we pull it up and over us in our safe place, and it provides the warmth we need. Or in the early morning when we have just made a cup of coffee, baked granny's favorite muffins, and opened God's Word, it's the best blanket to remind us of God's goodness and faithfulness. It's perfect for every season of our life.

Today's Slice of the Pie

▲ What words come to mind when you think of Christ's family quilt?

▲ Do you wonder why God put a certain relationship in your life?

▲ If you think about it, why do you think God brought that person to you? Would you be OK not knowing the answer? Why or why not?

▲ Do you need to open up your hands and surrender a relationship to God? Pray and ask God to help you do that right now.

▲ Who is someone you can reach out to today to encourage?

12

The Intersection of Love

"You shall love the Lord your God with all your heart, and with all your soul, and with all your mind." This is the great and foremost commandment.

MATTHEW 22:37–38 NASB

The greatest commandment is to love the Lord your God with all your heart, soul, and mind. Why is this so hard? First, we have to genuinely understand how great our Father's love is for us. It's hard to know that kind of love when we haven't received it here on earth. For many of us, lies have been spoken over us by those who claim to love us, and it can feel like we've been kicked and bruised. As hard as it is, we must remember that those people are coming from brokenness too. For others of us, we ask ourselves: *How can I love someone so deeply like Jesus when I can't even love myself?*

God wants nothing more than for us to sit at his feet, let him comb our hair, scratch our backs, and hold us when we fall. He wants us to crawl up in his lap and know what love is. He wants us to trust him and know that he sees us and has never left us. Even though it is hard, won't you let him love you? If you will, your heart, soul, and mind can begin to heal and transform into a beautyFULL story of redemption. Then, you can go share of his goodness, which is what The Great Commission is all about—pouring your heart, soul, and mind out to make disciples. Won't you sit at the intersection of the greatest commandment and The Great Commission and serve everyone a big ole slice of love, grace, and pie?

Today's Slice of the Pie

▲ What does it mean to you to love God with your heart, soul, and mind?

▲ How can you shift your perspective and begin living at the intersection of love?

▲ What does it mean to you to be loved by the Father?

13

Be the Girl

When you give to the needy, do not let your left hand know what your right hand is doing, so that your giving may be in secret. Then your Father, who sees what is done in secret, will reward you.

MATTHEW 6:1-4

Let's be real. We don't need any more friends who come alongside us and point out all our imperfections. We live in our heads and tell ourselves about them all the time. I have no desire to hear, "You should have done this" or "You're not doing it right." A true friend sees you in your brokenness, struggles, and hurting and comes along and helps without boasting or wanting something in return. We need more women who see our crowns falling off our heads in the grocery store while our baby is screaming from the cart and comes over to distract the baby then leans in and says, "You're doing a great job, Mama. I've been there. It isn't easy."

Be the girl who stops by when a friend is sick. Heck, don't even ask what she needs. Most likely, your girlfriend will feel like a burden and say she's all good. Show up anyway with dinner, empty the dishwasher, or put in a load of laundry. Take the kids out for ice cream. Just show up and do nothing. But be the girl who shows up wanting nothing in return, just ready to give love, kindness, and grace. Don't post it on social media looking for praise. Your girlfriend sees it and feels loved and seen, and our Father is watching. He is pleased.

a true friend fixes a friend's crown without saying a word

TODAY'S SLICE OF THE PIE

▲ Do you have a friend who comes alongside and fixes your crown when it's falling off? Who comes to mind?

▲ Today, how can you be the girl who fixes a friend's crown?

14

Savor and Feast

Be imitators of God, as beloved children. And walk in love, as Christ loved us and gave himself up for us, a fragrant offering and sacrifice to God.

EPHESIANS 5:1–2 ESV

I have loved gathering people for as long as I can remember. My parents instilled it in me growing up. My mom would decorate the table for every season. She even had a hutch full of dishes and would curate beautiful vignettes. My dad was usually the one in the kitchen cooking something simple but with great depth of flavor. We always had family dinner on Monday nights—sometimes it was just us; other times friends and family gathered. I'm so grateful that this gift was given to me at an early age, and it has carried over into every aspect of my life. With work, family, and friends. I love the whole process, from planning the menu, gathering the guests, and creating a safe space. Of course, I would usually go overboard on the food and have too much. I wanted everyone to be filled up, both physically and spiritually.

But now I see savoring and feasting differently. Now my table is rarely clean, dishes are piled in the sink, dirty socks and shoes are strewn all over the floor, and we might have grabbed a rotisserie chicken and

bagged salad from the grocery store for dinner. Savor means to relish in, to treasure fully. We don't have to create elaborate meals to savor our time together. Don't get me wrong. I love good food, but at times we seem to overcomplicate it and make it about more than the people. I want to not only savor the food, but I also genuinely want to savor the relationships. I want to look at family and friends face to face and make sure they know what a treasure they are to me and, more importantly, to Jesus. I want to feast on all his goodness and savor it with his people. I want to share my time and the gifts he's given me to create relationships. Do you ever think about the difference between savoring and feasting? It's kind of eye-opening when we begin to apply it to our lives, isn't it?

Today's Slice of the Pie

- ▲ What do you feast on too much?

- ▲ How can you turn that feasting into savoring?

- ▲ How could you gather a friend, a group of friends, or family to savor his favor this week?

Granny's Banana Nut Muffins

Yield: 14 muffins

Ingredients

1¾ cups flour
½ cup Crisco
1 teaspoon vanilla
7 tablespoons buttermilk
2 teaspoons baking powder
1½ cups sugar
3 eggs
1 cup mashed bananas
1 cup chopped pecans (optional)

Instructions

Preheat oven to 300°F. Grease two muffin pans.

Using an electric mixer, cream the Crisco, vanilla, eggs, and buttermilk in a large bowl until fluffy.

In a separate bowl, sift the flour and baking powder together. Add the milk and flour alternately to the creamed mixture until all is combined.

Fold in the mashed bananas and pecans.

Fill greased muffin pans to ¾ full. Bake for 30 to 35 minutes.

15

The Hills and Valleys of Pie Crust

He will sit as a refiner and purifier of silver,
and he will purify the sons of Levi and refine them like
gold and silver, and they will bring offerings
in righteousness to the Lord.

MALACHI 3:3 ESV

I love how we can use something as simple and everyday as a pie to share God's love. I think pie crust is a lovely example of his love. Think about it. The dips in the crust between the peaks around the outer edge, the ups and downs, his thumbprint creating it all. Picture yourself standing in your kitchen with Jesus right next to you. You dump the flour in the bowl and add the Crisco, slowly cutting the shortening in and adding texture to your life. You pour in the salt water.

Then, Jesus says, "Go slow, mix it well, but don't overdo it. It's OK if all the crumbs don't get mixed in. We don't need all the things of this world. Now form the dough into three balls. Look, it's the perfect foundation for a pie—and your life. Now, dust the counter and roll out one ball. It doesn't have to be perfectly round, but it's a circle of my never-ending love. Okay, let's put the crust in the pan and crimp the edges. Don't worry. I'm right here. There's so much grace for you. I know that you feel the crust has to be just like your grandma's, but that's not your crust. This is your crust. Now let's get back to crimping, creating the hills and valleys around the edge. Remember, I'll always be there, holding your hand while you walk through the hills and valleys. My fingerprint is on your life."

You speak up and say, "But Jesus, it doesn't look good!" And he answers, "Oh, child, but it does. It's perfectly imperfect, just like you. Now let us fill it with all your life experiences and bake it for a while." You pour in all your best ingredients into the firm foundation and place it in the fire. It bakes for a while, and slowly the ingredients melt together, and you continue to become one with him. His love is full of forgiveness and grace, and when you pull the pie out of the oven, it is beautiful and full of flavor, just like your life.

"My grace is sufficient for you, for my power is perfected in weakness."

TODAY'S SLICE OF THE PIE

▲ How did you feel as you imagined Jesus making the pie dough with you?

▲ Now, go back, close your eyes, and see him holding your hand through the hills and valleys of life. Go back to a season that was really hard and imagine him right there with you—because he was, the whole time.

▲ This week, think of other times you didn't feel his presence strongly in your life. Close your eyes and picture him there with you. Life is so much sweeter knowing he's walking alongside us through the good and the bad, isn't it?

16

God's Healing Balm

Grace and peace be yours in abundance through
the knowledge of God and of Jesus our Lord.

2 PETER 1:2

When we talk about our hearts being broken, what
does that look like to you? A spouse speaking words
that are gut-wrenching? A friend promising to meet
you for breakfast and then forgetting? The loss of a
child? The doctor confirming a disease? Can you feel
your heart fall into your stomach? My heart is cracked
and fractured from past hurts, and at times when I'm
in the dark, all it takes is a word or phrase to trigger
old feelings and memories, and suddenly those cracks
grow wider and deeper.

I'm going to share one of my triggers with you. I was previously married, and it was not a marriage rooted in love, Jesus, or grace. My ex-husband was an alcoholic, abuser, and cheated often. By the grace of God, I was taken out of that marriage and given Rick, the best husband ever! But the wounds from my past have taken a while to heal. For example, early in our marriage, whenever Rick went out with friends to have a drink, I would think the worst: *Is he cheating? Is he in jail? Did he have a wreck and die?* I lived in fear.

Slowly, God showed me that I could trust Rick. I poured love, hope, and peace into the broken parts of my heart. The cracks are still there, but now I see them differently; I see them healed by Jesus. He gave me a new song to sing—a song of his healing and restoration. You can recover from past hurts with his love, mercy, and grace. They're our only healing balm.

Today's Slice of the Pie

▲ Friend, what broken parts of your heart need healing by God's unending grace and peace?

▲ If you're not sure, won't you sit at his feet and let him show you what things trigger fear or hurt in you?

17

Hurtful Words

Speaking the truth in love, we will grow to become in every respect the mature body of Him who is the head, that is, Christ. From him the whole body joined and held together by every supporting ligament, grows and builds itself up in love, as each part does its work.

EPHESIANS 4:15–16

Some weeks are a struggle at our house with kids talking back and saying disrespectful and hurtful things. They are young and don't always know how to verbalize their feelings. I can remember an instance when hurtful words were spoken to me, and even though I knew they were not meant to be hurtful or on purpose, I heard them just the same. This can lead to me telling my children that I'm the boss or saying things out of anger and frustration. But when I think back on those situations, I am reminded that I need to meet them exactly where they are in their journey.

Speaking the truth in love isn't an easy thing. But why is it so hard? Many times, we completely avoid the situation and decide not to speak the truth at all. We ignore it with the hope that it will simply go away. Other times we talk about the truth but use daggers instead of love. Harsh words quickly fire out of our mouths, and before we realize it, we have wounded the other person, leaving each of us broken and on the floor.

What I have been learning and leaning into is this: if I speak the words that are on the tip of my tongue, the outcome should be healing. So, before I speak, I try to ask myself if healing will actually come from my words. In order to give myself time to think this through, I can't immediately speak the first thing that comes to

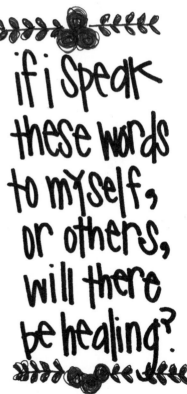

if i Speak these words to myself, or others, will there be healing?

mind. I must first be still. I have to stop myself, sit in it, rest in it, and ask Jesus if he even wants me to speak. Sometimes he doesn't; instead, he may want me to be quiet and rely on him. That's not easy, especially in the heat of a battle. In those moments, I have to ask myself: *If Jesus were sitting right next to me, would he be cheering me on? Or would he be sad?* Argh! Yep, the truth is, many times I'm speaking from past feelings and emotions, and that rarely has a good outcome! My words should be spoken in truth and love. That's when God can use my words to be a healing salve.

Today's Slice of the Pie

▲ Think of a situation where you spoke hurtful words to someone. Were you being mindful of what you said, or were you reacting out of hurt or anger?

▲ Practice breathing and reflecting this week before you speak. Is there a question or a phrase that you can use to remind yourself to think first?

▲ Ask yourself this question: Do I respond, react, or speak with purpose? If not, from whom do I need to ask forgiveness?

▲ Does being quiet and silent come easy, or is it something that is hard for you?

18

A Life-giving Narrative

Jesus said to him, "Get up! Pick up your mat
and walk." At once the man was cured;
he picked up his mat and walked.

JOHN 5:1–9

I had never heard life compared to a damaged
narrative until a dear friend spoke about it at an event.
I quickly understood what she meant because I once
spoke a damaged tale over my own life. I played the
victim and pity game very well. I could coin a sentence
to manipulate a situation and get what I wanted by
guilting someone. My hurts were deep from trying to
please others in the workplace. I carried guilt from
believing that all the bad things happening to my

family members were my fault because of the position I held in our family business. Owning and running a family business is one of the hardest things. Your family comes to you for decisions, and there is usually someone who doesn't agree. Being a people pleaser, I would please them and not stand in truth. I had given my power away and was left powerless, even though I was in control of our business.

I didn't pick running the family business; it chose me because of circumstances and decisions that other people made. My relationship with my parents was painful. Harsh words were spoken about me to others, and they turned their backs on me. We were doing nothing but tearing each other down. The only way out was to remove myself from the situation, and God made a way for that. He took me and my husband out of the café, and through stillness, prayer, and a tribe that spoke life-giving words over us, I began to heal. I began to see that all the words spoken over me were a lie, and I was not a victim. I did have a choice. I always did.

I can say yes and I can say no when I'm standing in God's best and his truth. I must stand in knowing that he is the only approval that I need. No one else's really matters. Other people's thoughts about me are none of my business. I didn't have to be a victim. My narrative can be a life-giving one. And now I can see that I have a story to share with others who are living in a world where they feel powerless and play the victim. Jesus has healed us and wants us to be complete from the inside out. He wants us to be able to see the world with different options, choices, and ways out! He has given you free will. Be a victor in your story! You were made to be victorious through him! Life isn't happening to you; it's happening for you.

Today's Slice of the Pie

▲ What part of your life are you speaking a damaged narrative over?

▲ Where might you be feeling trapped and playing the victim? Pray and ask God to show you a way out.

▲ How can your damaged narrative be rewritten to become life-giving?

Be the girl that speaks lifegiving truth over yourself, family & friends.

Sweet 'n' Salty Pie

Yield: 2 pies

INGREDIENTS

2 1-pound Royers dough balls
½ cup butter • 1½ cups sugar
2 eggs • 2 teaspoons vanilla
1 cup flour • ⅓ cup cocoa powder
⅓ teaspoon baking soda • ¼ teaspoon salt
¾ cup Kraft caramel bits • ½ cup chocolate chips
¼ tsp sea salt

INSTRUCTIONS

Preheat oven to 350°F.

Roll out a dough ball and place into a 9-inch pie pan to form a pie shell.

In a large bowl, beat the butter, sugar, eggs, and vanilla until the mixture is light and fluffy.

In a separate bowl, combine the flour, cocoa powder, baking soda, and salt.

Stir the flour mixture into the butter mixture until well blended.

Mix in the caramel bits and chocolate chips.

Pack the filling into the pie shell and sprinkle with sea salt.

Bake at 350°F for 35 to 45 minutes.

If your knife doesn't come out clean, it's OK!

19

Protect Your Peace

Guard your heart above all else,
for it determines the course of your life.

PROVERBS 4:23 NLT

What does it truly mean to protect your peace? For many years I believed it meant to build a wall to hide behind and protect yourself from harm, both spiritually and physically. But all that did was create division and death. Hiding didn't solve any of the problems in front of me. I had to learn to tear down the wall and build a cute white picket fence with space for beauty to grow and bloom. When a weed began to take root, I could pick it out.

As friends and family walked along the other side of the fence, I got to decide if I wanted to open

the gate or not to let them in. The fence wasn't too high that I couldn't see over it. If the person on the other side of the fence was someone who built me up spiritually, respected my weaknesses, and didn't take advantage of them, then I could invite them in to enjoy a cup of coffee or a slice of pie. But if they didn't truly respect me and couldn't build me up, then I could just wave at them and continue tending my garden, loving them from the opposite side of the fence.

Once we recognize the lie that we have to agree with everything our friends or family members say, we can have a healthy relationship. We don't have to compromise our beliefs to love someone. We can love that person just as they are. We just have to let Jesus shine through us and let him do the work. Friend, won't you tear down the wall and begin to let the light shine through your fence?

Today's Slice Of the Pie

- ▲ Are there walls in your life that you have built that don't allow for any growth or light to shine in? What are those?

- ▲ What would it look like to knock that wall down and build a picket fence with room for growth and the light to shine in?

- ▲ Who specifically do you need to create healthy boundaries with so that God can turn a damaged relationship into a healed one?

20

God Is My Business Plan

Whatever you ask for in prayer, believe that you have received it, and it will be yours.

MARK 11: 24

I was the girl who did everything she could to get out of taking the SAT. Standardized testing paralyzed me. As graduation and college were approaching, I found out that I didn't have to take the SAT if I went to the local community college. But even knowing that, I was stuck in the lie that I was not smart enough for college. So, I stayed behind and worked in our family business. Looking back, I think I learned more about life working in the café than I ever would have in college. I look at the mistakes I made as experiences and not failures.

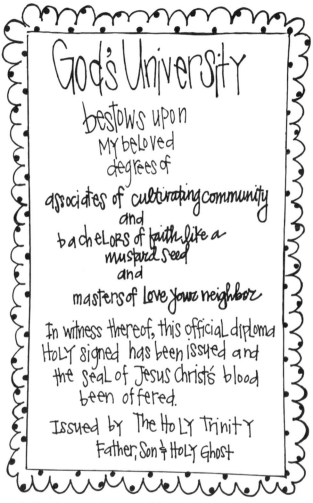

God's University

bestows upon
My beloved
degrees of

associates of cultivating community
and
bachelors of faith like a
mustard seed
and

masters of Love your neighbor

In witness thereof, this official diploma
Holy signed has been issued and
the seal of Jesus Christ's blood
been offered.

Issued by The Holy Trinity
Father, Son & Holy Ghost

I didn't fail; I learned something.

Over the years, as our family business has grown
and expanded, I've never been one to create business
plans or marketing strategies. When we needed a loan,

I went to God. He is my boss. He is my banker. He is my business plan. I knew that when I walked into the bank, he was already making a way, and if the door shut, I just needed to pivot and look at it a different way. He had gotten us this far in business, and he wasn't going to leave us now. Through the years I've been able to see that my thesis for life is to gather people through Jesus, pie, and coffee. It could be through a book, an event, dinner in a field, or an illustration on social media. I don't want to miss out on my daily work with the Lord. I want to be the best employee ever.

P.S. A couple of years ago, my dad gave me a diploma he made for me. It's from "The Prestigious Patriarchal School of Dad's Business School at Royers Round Top Café." It's better than any state funded or private college diploma I could've received, and it's still hanging in our home to remind me just how far I've come.

Today's Slice of the Pie

▲ Have you ever pictured God as your boss? If you were watching your life on the TV show *Undercover Boss* and God was the boss, what do you think he would tell you?

▲ Today, if you shifted your perspective and saw your job as working for God, how would you show up to work differently?

21

Red Polka-Dot Tankini

The Lord said to Samuel, "Do not look on his appearance or on the height of his stature, because I have rejected him. For the Lord sees not as man sees: man looks on the outward appearance, but the Lord looks on the heart."

1 Samuel 16:7 esv

Growing up in Texas, you better love the heat or at least get used to it! For years, I didn't like the summer because I was consumed with my body image and worried about what everyone else was thinking about me. I wouldn't wear shorts or sleeveless shirts, and I would cover myself up so you couldn't see my legs or arms—you know, the ones that Granny passed down.

Some people call them chalkboard arms, but I call them angel wings. Anyway, I was suffocating from all the lies I believed about my body and all the clothes I used to cover everything up. I only wore swimsuits that sucked it all in. They had to be black and something my granny could borrow. I would then cover that up with shorts and a shirt.

I remember the days that words about my body image were spoken over me and changed my view

She wore it anyway and loved herself

of myself. There was the time I was running across highway 237 from our café to our house and a boy a year older than me yelled from the gas station, "Look at that fat girl run!" Or the time when a boy told me, "If you were only skinnier, I would date you." That was thirty-two years ago, and I remember those words like they were spoken yesterday.

The hurtful words don't sting so much anymore as I've come to learn that my size doesn't make me who I am on the inside. I love myself for me. I love myself because God created me, and he gave me free will to eat ice cream with my kiddos. He's also given me free will to make healthier choices, and I have. I now wear the cutest red and white polka-dot tankini and get the craziest number of compliments. Those are the words I remember now. "Oh, my goodness! You look precious." In the end, that's all that matters—that I know what my Father thinks of me, and I'm precious in his eyes.

Today's Slice of the Pie

▲ If you have struggled with this, reflect on a time someone said something about your weight or body and it stuck with you. How did it make you feel about yourself?

▲ Now, reflect on how God sees you. Write down five words that he uses to describe you and soak them up. Use them to remind yourself of who you really are.

22

Being Still

Seek first his kingdom and his righteousness,
and all these things will be given to you as well.

MATTHEW 6:33

I am the oldest child of four with three younger
brothers. My brothers called me Mother Hen when
we were growing up. All I knew was busy. Working,
working, working. Checking things off that long to-do
list that was never done—never! I thought doing things
meant I was accomplishing something, doing something
with my life, and earning my earthly family's love. I
was always saying yes to events, being the persistent
entrepreneur, and starting new businesses with the
hopes of earning more money. I would check the bank

account over and over to make sure there was plenty of money just to cover expenses. There were times when it didn't matter how hard I worked; there just wasn't enough money. I didn't realize it at the time, but money was quickly becoming my idol. I checked the bank account like people check their text messages. Of course, God was watching the whole time, and he always provided.

Now, God has my family in a season of change. God has taken my husband and me out of our last four jobs, and I have to admit, that was a hard transition. It's taken me nearly three years to start slowing down to realize that my job right now is to be still with him. A dream job! I've finally reached a point where I can actually enjoy this season of quiet, of being still, and digging my roots deeper in him. More importantly, I know the benefit! Being still has allowed me to focus on my past and take the time to process it. Being still *is* productive! Yes, it is hard work to see him in everything, to walk by faith and not by sight, to be still, to press into him and trust that he has woven the threads of my story together for what is in front of me.

Today's Slice of the Pie

- ▲ In Hebrew, being still means letting go. What are you trying to control? Can you really fix it?

- ▲ What stops you from being still?

- ▲ What can you do today to stop and make God the first thing on your to-do list?

Louise's Herb Mix and Pie Crust

Herb Mix

Yield: 3 cups

1 cup garlic powder (not garlic salt)
⅔ cup dill weed
⅓ cup marjoram
⅓ cup dried basil leaves
⅓ cup dried thyme leaves
⅛ cup course ground black pepper
Pinch of cayenne pepper

Mix ingredients in a bowl and store in an air-tight container. You may want to wear a face mask; you will be sneezing!

This is so good on roasted veggies!

Herb Pie Crust

Yield: 3 1-pound dough balls

INGREDIENTS

¼ tsp salt
1 cup water
5 cups white flour
2 cups Crisco shortening
4 teaspoons herb mix

INSTRUCTIONS

Dissolve the salt in the water and set aside.

Cut the Crisco and 4 teaspoons of herb mix into the flour with a fork or pastry cutter. When the mixture is crumbly, add the salt water and knead until the water is absorbed.

Add several tablespoons of flour and continue to knead the dough until it pulls cleanly away from your hands. Roll the dough into three separate balls and place each of them in a plastic bag and freeze until you are ready to use them.

When you are ready to use the dough, set it out to thaw for 3 to 4 hours or place in your refrigerator to thaw overnight.

The dough rolls out easiest at room temperature.

Now, bake your favorite savory pie!

23

Narrow Gate

Enter through the narrow gate.
For wide is the gate
and broad is the road
that leads to destruction,
and many enter through it.
But small is the gate
and narrow the road
that leads to life,
and only a few to find it.

MATTHEW 7:13–14 NIV

We have experienced many painful moments in our lives recently. The hardest part of walking through hard times is stopping and listening to what God wants us to learn from these experiences. At church, our pastor once spoke on the narrow gate and the wide gate. I'm a visual girl, and this has helped me navigate life's curve balls. It's so much easier to take the wide gate: one too many cookies or Italian margaritas, too many hours scrolling through Instagram and Facebook, or maybe spending too much time on a relationship that isn't life-giving. That last one might be one of the hardest blind spots to see because you want to believe the best in everyone. You want to believe people are on your side, but if you were honest with yourself, you'd agree that they aren't building you up.

It's easier to cover-up our pains and numb out with the world by entering through the wide gate than it is to enter the narrow gate and dive into Jesus. When we walk through the narrow gate, he is right there with exactly what you need. He is there to help you dig out of the pain and stop numbing it with the things that the wide gate offers. Jesus is on the other side of the narrow gate. His arms are wide open. Won't you enter through it?

Today's Slice of the Pie

▲ What in your life keeps you walking through the wide gate?

▲ What can you do today to focus on the narrow gate?

24

Jesus Isn't a Marketing Tool

Do not fear, for I have redeemed you; I have summoned you by name; you are mine. When you pass through the waters, I will be with you; and when you pass through the rivers, they will not sweep over you. When you walk through the fire, you will not be burned; the flames will not set you ablaze. For I am the Lord your God, the Holy One of Israel, your Savior.

ISAIAH 43:1-3

I was once told by a close friend, "Jesus isn't a marketing tool in business." Since this was said by

What kind of utensil are You for the kingdom of God? a knife, chopping away at life & people, never looking up? or a spoon? scooping & pouring goodness in Your bowl that overflows into others. A spoon that is washed & rinsed in his water & set in the cabinet to rest before You serve again

someone that I looked up to and trusted, I started to second-guess myself. Do *I* use Jesus as a marketing tool? But I think that's precisely what the enemy wanted me to do: second-guess myself. I stopped my train of thought and stood in my truth. No, Jesus isn't a marketing tool; I am *his* marketing tool. I am the one he picked to share about him through pie, relationships, writing his Word on the walls, and not being scared to speak his name to a customer, no matter what they might believe.

It makes me think of the song "This Is Your Time" by Michael W. Smith, which was about Cassie Bernall who was killed in the Columbine school shooting. She shined. She shared about Jesus, and God used the loss of her life for those left here on earth. She was dancing with Jesus while everyone here on earth was grieving her loss. God used a song, relationships, and bagpipes to comfort the family and let them know that he was near. How are you allowing Jesus to use you as his marketing tool? Are you afraid or embarrassed to speak his name to those you don't know? Or are you so proud of his name and what he has done for you that you don't care what others think?

Today's Slice of the Pie

▲ What marketing tool has God given you to further his kingdom?

▲ Do you use it without fear or are you too embarrassed?

▲ How can you go out and use it today or this week?

25

All our Junk

There is a time for everything, and a season for every activity under the heavens: a time to be born and a time to die, a time to plant and a time to uproot, a time to kill and a time to heal, a time to tear down and a time to build, a time to weep and a time to laugh, a time to mourn and a time to dance, a time to scatter stones and a time to gather them, a time to embrace and a time to refrain from embracing, a time to search and a time to give up, a time to keep and a time to throw away, a time to tear and a time to mend, a time to be silent and a time to speak, a time to love and a time to hate, a time for war and a time for peace.

ECCLESIASTES 3:1–8

I'm still in awe of how God has used pie to teach me so many lessons. Take Royers Junkberry Pie. One day we decided to take everything leftover from our other fruit pies and combine it to make one big delicious super pie, the Junkberry. The name comes from some local friends of ours over at Junk Gypsy. They love fruit pies. So we thought, *Why not name a pie after them?* After all, this pie does contain all the leftover junk from our kitchen.

   The Junkberry Pie is tart, sweet, rich in color,

messy, and full of goodness—just like our tangled lives. Now let's fill it with the love of Jesus, and you have a beautiful, glorious mess. The crust reminds me of Jesus' arms, holding all our junk together. When I think life is too tart or the season is too hard, I know that he is holding me up and making something new, all in his timing. There is a time for everything in our lives. Everything works together for our good and his glory, right?

Lord knows that I don't like surrendering everything to him (I might have control issues). But just like we took all the leftover fruit, even things that didn't make sense, and turned it into something sweet, I can surrender all my junk to Jesus. And when I do, when I'm willing to let go of everything, I get a life that is sometimes a little tart, a little messy, full of things that don't make sense, but in the end, full of goodness and oh, so sweet.

Today's Slice of the Pie

▲ What junk do you have in your life?

▲ Why is it so hard to surrender it to God?

▲ What has he made new in your life recently?

Junkberry Pie

Yield: 2 pies

INGREDIENTS

2 1-pound Royers dough balls

FILLING INGREDIENTS

¾ cup sugar
½ cup flour
2 cups peeled, cored,
and cubed Granny Smith apples
1 cup frozen blueberries
½ cup frozen raspberries
1 cup frozen strawberries
½ cup frozen peaches
1 cup frozen blackberries

TOPPING INGREDIENTS

1 cup sour cream
1 tablespoon salt
¾ cup flour
1 cup sugar

Instructions

Preheat oven to 350°F.

Roll out a dough ball and place into a 9-inch pie pan to form a pie shell.

Add the strawberries and peaches to a large pan.

Pile the remaining fruit on top.

Heat until the fruit begins to soften, stirring often.

Add in the sugar and flour and continue to stir.

Once the fruit has softened (it doesn't have to be boiling or hot!), remove it from the heat and set aside.

Combine all the topping ingredients in a mixer and beat until smooth.

Fill each 9-inch pie shell with fruit filling and top with sour cream topping.

Sprinkle with sugar and bake for 50 minutes or until topping is golden brown.

26

What Are You Cultivating?

Count it all as joy, my brothers, when you meet trials
of various kinds, for you know that the testing of your
faith produces steadfastness. And let steadfastness
have its full effect, that you may be perfect and
complete, lacking in nothing.

JAMES 1:2-4 ESV

I used to cultivate a lot of things in my garden. I
wanted all the pretty flowers and vegetables, and
I would cram it all in. As much as I could fit into
the space, I would shove it all in there. I liked a full
garden—overflowing! I didn't follow the directions that
said to space plants twelve inches apart. I'd barely
leave any room for them to grow properly; then they

would eventually choke each other out. Then, I'd just stop tending to them completely. My garden had become too much work for me. There were other more important day to day things that were now demanding my attention, and I could not find the time to make my garden pretty again. I just let everything in it die. I didn't water anything. I didn't fertilize anything. I also didn't make an effort to stop and learn what needed to be done in order to make it grow again.

cultivate Your Best Life

So, here I am, starting a new garden in my life. The old beds have been cleared out and made ready, and this time I'm planting what and how God wants me to plant. He wants me to cultivate the things I know to be true. I have worked hard and weeded out what is not of him, and now I'm only going to grow what is of him, things like peace, truth, joy, and other life-giving things. And, when the stinky stuff (fertilizer) is needed for growth, and it always is, I will react differently because of faith. I will cry out to him and ask what he wants me to learn from this. I may be a blubbering mess while I'm asking him questions, but I'll ask anyway. *Why do I have to do that? Why can't I have that? Why can't things be this way instead?* However, this time I'll know to only look to him for the answers to those questions. And I will understand that growth is happening no matter what and he will give me answers in time. I will be faithful.

He will always provide the tools to cultivate our best lives. A song on the radio, a simple word from a friend, an unsolicited kind voice memo or text. My human flesh sometimes wants to cultivate things my way. But only he is enough, and when we cultivate what is his best for us, we will have all we need, and we'll want for nothing. My garden is abundant. It is a beautiful joy-filled life. It's full of resting at his feet, weeding out earthly desires, sitting with the broken, and enjoying my beautiful home, family, friends, and ministry. He is all I ever needed.

Today's Slice of the Pie

- ▲ What are you cultivating right now?

- ▲ What things do you need to weed out to start anew?

- ▲ What do you want your garden to look like?

27

Not How I Wanted to Celebrate

See what great love the Father has lavished on us, that we should be called children of God!

1 John 3:1 NIV

I love to celebrate—the big things like birthdays, anniversaries, and milestones as well as the small things.

It was coming up on our thirteenth wedding anniversary, and Rick said we just couldn't afford to go away for a few days. I dreamed of going places we haven't been to, wandering the streets, and planning our days around where we were going to eat. Then the day came and we didn't have anything planned, and I was OK with it. The morning went as usual, and Rick went to his early morning Bible study. But before he left, he gave me a card and a 3 Musketeers® bar. To

be honest, I was really excited because I hadn't had a 3 Musketeers® or even sugar like that in a long time! But as I looked at the 3 Musketeers® bar, I was reminded of the Father, the Son, and the Holy Spirit and how the Trinity holds our family together.

Once Rick got back home, we dropped the kids off at school then went to Starbucks for coffee. That was our date. We talked about budgets. Yippee! Then Rick started sharing things that were on his heart. He said he wanted us to get back to sitting around the table and sharing time together as a family. He said he realized that it needed to start with him leading everything in our home. Spiritually, financially, how he communicates to me in front of the kids, and how he shows teamwork at home. No more hitting the snooze button in the mornings. He even cooks breakfast sometimes—all the praise hands!

Later that day, I was delivering some catering, and our oldest son, Brayden, said he wanted to come with me to take it and set it up. He got in the car and said, "Mom, I didn't bring my iPad® so we can talk!" And then he asked if we could take the back roads because "there's always something interesting or exciting that way." This mama's heart was filled up.

I thought I needed to go on a romantic getaway with Rick to celebrate that day, but what I really needed was to celebrate at home. We did that, and God showed up big in how he lavished his love on me that day. He made it clear that what I needed was a candy bar, a coffee date over budgets, hearing Rick's heart, and talking with my oldest to celebrate this milestone—not a fancy getaway. I will hold that day close in my heart and pull the treasures out when I need to be reminded of his faithfulness. And I will never be able to look at a 3 Musketeers® bar again and not think of the holy Trinity.

Today's Slice of the Pie

▲ Has there been something in your life recently that didn't go how you wanted it to go?

▲ How did God lavish his love on you even in your disappointment?

▲ In what ways did you celebrate his goodness and faithfulness?

28

The Right Ingredients

You will know the truth,
and the truth will set you free.

JOHN 8:32

Imagine you're in the kitchen and have a bunch of
different ingredients on the counter to make the best
pie you've ever made. Some are extra ingredients, and
others wouldn't taste right in a pie. Now imagine that
the pie you're making is your life and you get to fill
your pie with the ingredients that you want. For many
years, I poured the wrong ingredients into my life. I was
scooping in bitterness, anger, shame, blame, and guilt
by the cupful. I believed everything was my fault and
that I was the bad one. Hard things happened, and I

keep tweaking the recipe
'til it's filled with
HIS best ingredients

forgiveness
hope
mercy   love
truth grace self-con

spoke lies over my life to make sense of it all. It's easier
to believe lies over truth, isn't it? I thought I was adding
truth to my pie, but through much hard work, I found

out I was filling my pie with things that kept leaving a bad taste in my mouth. What a mess!

When we pour the wrong ingredients into our lives, we don't look so beautiful on the outside or the inside. We look crumbled and cracked; we lose our light, and our sparkle is gone. Do you know how to tell the difference between the truth or a lie? Truth is light, and lies are dark. The light helps you see things for what they truly are. In the dark you are left feeling around and trying to figure things out. But the good news is that even in a dark room, he is always there. Truth makes you feel real, authentic, equipped, powerful, and encouraged. Lies leave you feeling fake, unequipped, powerless, and discouraged. God doesn't see you that way, and he definitely doesn't want you to feel that way. He has given you the ingredients to be free—hope, grace, mercy, love, peace, and joy. Put those ingredients into your life and see how things taste!

TODAY'S SLICE OF THE PIE

▲ What ingredients are you pouring into your life?

▲ List five things, or as many as you like, that you are tired of believing about yourself.

▲ Now, list the opposite of those lies. Don't those words feel more like truth to you?

29

Stay in Your Lane

"For I know the plans I have for you," declares the Lord, "plans to prosper you and not to harm you, plans to give you hope and a future."

Jeremiah 29:11

Remember when we didn't have social media waving at us 24/7? When the only way to communicate was by picking up the phone, sending a letter, or visiting face to face? Oh boy, it sure was a lot easier to stay in your lane, right? Fewer distractions? The only way we knew someone got married, had a baby, got a new job, or colored their hair was by a phone call, an invitation, or seeing them at church or the grocery! These days we know what everyone else is doing every day, hour, or, for some, minute. We scroll one more time or just a few minutes longer to see what they had for lunch, what cute shoes they bought, how they just remodeled their whole house, or what fantastic trip they just took! All this scrolling can sometimes lead to a little bit of jealousy, right? Everyone's life looks so great from a filtered, curated, social media perspective.

The problem is, when we spend so much time looking at other people's lives, we can start to drift out of the lane God has placed us in. The lane I'm in right now is entirely different from any other road I've traveled. It's a path of being still and learning what that looks like in Jesus. I don't need a perfectly clean house, to make a ton of money, or to dress in a cute, new outfit. This lane is showing me that the things of the past are not in front of me and that I must learn from those things but not carry them forward. They weren't mistakes, just experiences that I can grow from. He is teaching me to keep showing up, moving forward, and stop picking up the things of the past. Those things aren't mine anymore.

We must learn to cheer each other on from our own lanes! When we cross into someone else's lane, there's a good chance a collision will happen. We can run alongside each other and encourage one another. In fact, when we run fully in our own lane, the lane God put us in, we can push each other to be better because we are all working in the strengths and gifts God has given us. Is there any better place to be?

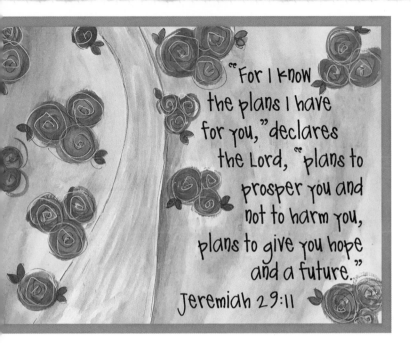

"For I know the plans I have for you," declares the Lord, "plans to prosper you and not to harm you, plans to give you hope and a future."

Jeremiah 29:11

TODAY'S SLICE OF THE PIE

▲ When you scroll through social media, where does your mind go when you see someone else's feed?

▲ Do you feel excited for them? Cheer them on? Or do you sit in jealousy a bit?

▲ What is God teaching you in the lane you're in right now? Are you following the path God has for you, or are you tempted to veer into someone else's lane?

30

Trust the Process

The vision awaits its appointed time; it hastens to the
end—it will not lie. If it seems slow, wait for it;
it will surely come; it will not delay.

HABAKKUK 2:3 ESV

Trusting the process slows me down and keeps me
from manipulating things to work how I want them
to, which, in the end, is not his best for me. Through
the season of Royers Round Top Café and Royers
Pie Haven, I've learned so much about trusting the
process. God would open a door, and I would rush
in and immediately do things my way. I didn't seek
wise counsel, sit in prayer, or trust what my heart was
saying. I believed what my selfish mind was saying.

trust
the
process

I wanted to know the next step and what the future held. I've learned over the years to slow my steps and, when God opens a door, to follow his lead, my feet safely stepping in his footsteps.

We have a big pie opportunity in front of us, and I can look toward the future and plan a bit, but there isn't any need to jump until God says to. I don't know the answers, and that's okay. We can ask questions, and we might not get a response. He knows the answer and will tell us as soon as we need to know. There is no more need to work late into the night to do more than

I'm called to do. Instead, I'm going to cherish that time and snuggle with my boys. I'm going to keep taking steps forward, lean into him, and wait for his lead. Friend, the pressure is off when we surrender to him and trust the process in everything. Do you know the song "While I Wait" by Lincoln Brewster? It's one of my favorites. Lean in and listen. Trusting the process takes time. This significant project we are working toward is a miracle only from God, and I know it will take time, but, in the end, it will be more than I could have ever imagined. He has the same thing in store for you!

Today's Slice of the Pie

▲ Where can you slow down and trust the process?

▲ What questions in your life do you think you need an answer to?

▲ What if you don't get the answer you want? Then what?

▲ What are the big pie opportunities in your own life? And do you believe that God will lead you to them?

Tara's Shepherd's Pie

Yield: 1 9-inch pie

INGREDIENTS

1 1-pound herb dough ball

FILLING

1½ pounds ground beef
2 teaspoons Lawry's lemon pepper
2 teaspoons garlic powder

VEGETABLE FILLING

1 cup fresh broccoli
¾ cup fresh carrots
½ cup fresh green peas
½ cup red onions, chopped
5 tablespoons dill butter
2 teaspoons fresh chopped rosemary

TOPPING

3 pounds russet potatoes, unpeeled
1 packet dry ranch dressing mix
16 ounces sour cream
1 cup shredded cheddar cheese

Preheat oven to 350°F.

Roll out the dough ball and place into a 9-inch pan to form a pie shell.

Mix the ground beef, salt, garlic powder, and lemon pepper in a bowl.

Place a large skillet over medium-high heat. Add the beef mixture and cook until browned. Set aside.

In a separate bowl, mix the vegetables, dill butter, and rosemary, then add it to the meat mixture.

Place the potatoes in a large pot and add enough water to cover them. Bring to a boil and cook until the potatoes are soft, using a fork to test for doneness. Drain the potatoes and return to the pot. (Potatoes can be made ahead of time if you'd like.)

Mash the potatoes and add the sour cream and ranch dry mix.

Fill the pie shell with the meat and vegetable filling, then pile on the mashed potatoes and press to cover the filling. Bake for 45 minutes, then remove pie from the oven.

Sprinkle the top with cheddar cheese and bake for an additional 5 minutes or until cheddar is melted.

31

Soul Restoration

He must increase,
but I must decrease.

JOHN 3:30 ASV

Our world adds layers to our life. We were created in the image of God, then the world gets in the way and we begin to add layers to cover up our hurts, faults, and pain. It's easier to cover up our bodies so that no one sees our scars. We add layers of makeup to cover our dark circles. We add hair color to cover the gray. We shove those hurtful words deep down and say, "I'm fine." We are like an old piece of furniture that has been passed around from one owner to the next. One adds a layer of paint. Another adds a shiny varnish to make it shine again. We do it in our homes as well. We buy more things to cover our walls and satisfy that desire to have all the things the rest of the world has.

What we really need to do is shed the layers. We need to simplify our lives. We need to clean out our souls from all the layers the world has added—the guilt, shame, and lies. We must strip back the layers to who we were initially created to be. Just like the original creator of that piece of furniture. He didn't create it to be passed around and continually covered in paint. He created it to give pleasure in its original condition. God created you the same way. Free of all the guilt, shame, betrayal, darkness, and pain. Let's get back to the original you—the time your soul was pure. When you take time to sit in your hurts and allow God to work in those places, your soul begins to heal, and the rest of your life becomes simple and clear. You see that saying no more and yes less is what works best for you because it creates space for you to dig deep and do the hard work of simplifying your soul. Just like with our homes: when we have cleared out all the clutter, our homes are easier to keep clean. The same is true for our souls.

Remember, God created you, and he doesn't want to leave you in pain. Sit with him, meditate back to that painful time, and ask him what he has for you? He wants to tell you. Let him become more in your life so you can go out and share more about his goodness and redemption.

▲ What do you need to strip back in your life or say no to? Could it be the way you spend time and money on your physical appearance, clothing, shopping, or home projects?

▲ How is your soul doing? Are there lies you're still believing?

▲ Are there areas of your life that you have shoved into your "soul closet" and need to declutter?

32

Waste Nothing

When they had all had enough to eat, he said to his
disciples, "Gather the pieces that are left over. Let
nothing be wasted." So, they gathered them and filled
twelve baskets with the pieces of the five barley loaves
left over by those who had eaten.

JOHN 6:10–13

After thirty years of working in my family's restaurant
business, I began to feel God nudging me onto a
different path. When I started thinking of work beyond
the restaurant world, I wondered, who in the world
would hire me? I didn't want to work for someone
else. I had done that once before, and it only lasted
for three days. I surely didn't want to work in another

restaurant. The restaurant business is hard work and requires crazy hours!

My mind was completely closed off to any other opportunities. I was only focusing on what was directly in front of me at this time. I honestly thought that I only had one set of skills, which included cooking, baking, and managing a restaurant. But God was busy doing so much more for me. Only God could have taken what I had experienced over the last thirty years in the hospitality world and gently pushed me to do something new with it—something I could have never imagined before. He was taking my pain and insecurity of the past and shining a big bright light into the future.

Just as I was transitioning out of working at the café, I went to a retreat called Soul Restoration. I needed a break and some rest, and I thought I was heading into the mountains of Idaho for some much-needed quiet time. Instead, God had signed me up for a retreat that was all about the healing and restoration of my old broken soul. He opened brand-new doors while showing me the truth about myself. He graciously helped me see that I was made for so much more and to understand that I do have a story to share with others. In fact, this is exactly what I was created to do in life! I was created to gather other people through food, love, and truth. Our God wastes nothing!

Today's Slice of the Pie

▲ Can you think of something in your life that you thought was a waste of your time? What was it?

▲ What did you learn from it?

▲ How did God take that and use it for your benefit and his glory?

33

Crushing and Pruning

Trust in the Lord with all your heart and lean not on your understanding; in all your ways submit to him, and he will make your paths straight. Do not be wise in your own eyes; fear the Lord and shun evil. This will bring health to your body and nourishment to your bones.

PROVERBS 3:5-8

There are days when I struggle and feel like everything I do is wrong. I begin to question my purpose. For me, that is what happens when I lose sight of my faith and let the world take over my thoughts. I begin to question the things that I do on a normal basis and wonder if I should be creating new product to sell. Then I question my abilities and ask myself, *Who would buy it?* I tell the Lord I created new content and classes, but no one has signed up. Did I do it for the wrong reasons? I must have. I didn't ask him. I just did it without God's *Heck yes!*

Why do I go off on my own and do the things I've always done? Did I do it to try to bring in money for my family? Or did I do it because I crave community and want to grow God's kingdom? In my experience, I tend to do things that I'm not supposed to when I feel our finances tightening and think I can fix it.

A friend once shared that we need to give away all that God has given us. We need to take all the gifts he has lavished upon us and all the life experiences he has taught us and share them with everyone. Then, we let him do the rest. When I'm sharing with others and focusing on him as the prize, I'm completely satisfied. But there are days when I want to crawl into a hole and keep it all to myself. Those are the days I know exactly where I am supposed to be—at his feet.

When I'm struggling and off track I must drop to my knees and cry out to him. He's the only one who can give you peace in the crushing and the pruning. Right now, he is pruning and crushing and creating wine. Wine takes a long time to ferment. You could drink the wine after twelve days, but it won't taste good. It takes a year to get good wine, but even then, it's still not the best. If you let it sit, it keeps getting better with each year that passes. So, I will continue to rest in him. I will evaluate what is good in my life right now, what needs to be pruned, and what isn't producing good fruit. And I will know that he is doing a new thing. It's not easy, but I will continually run to him to fulfill his purpose through me.

Today's Slice of the Pie

▲ When you are struggling with your purpose and place, what is the first place you go to? Do you go to God first or do you try to figure things out on your own?

▲ What is God showing you right now about pruning?

▲ What new wine is he crushing for you?

34

Fruits of the Spirit and Pie

The fruit of the Spirit is love, joy, peace, forbearance, kindness, goodness, faithfulness, gentleness and self-control. Against such things there is no law.

GALATIANS 5:22–23

Baking protects my heart and fills my mind and soul. It is a time when I can take refuge in him and pour out of myself and into food. It's a chance for me to be creative and try new recipes and know that I was created for such a time as this. It's a time to dream up fresh pies and food that connect people to Jesus. It's just Jesus and me in the kitchen, cooking and creating something good to share with the world. Baking reminds me of all the attributes of the fruits of the spirit and how we are to live in his Spirit in community. Below are some of the attributes that come to my mind.

Love – Pour your heart into making the pie. It will fill you and others up.

Joy – Baking brings joy to you and our Father when we do it out of selfless service. It brings happiness when we humbly bake a pie for someone. And when you knock on their door, the sweet fragrance of brown sugar and apples brings them back to a memory with Granny.

Peace – We need to learn to put down the to-do list and create. It brings peace, and we were created by the creator to create! We all have something that we are good at creating!

Patience – When we go slow and are patient, we are less likely to miss a step or ingredient. If we rush the baking process, our food is undercooked and sloppy, or we don't let the pie cool long enough, and it falls apart. Just like our lives, we must be patient with ourselves and the process.

Kindness – Serve yourself a slice of pie. Be kind to yourself, and it will flow to everyone around you.

Goodness – Fill the pie with all the good things: apples, strawberries, peaches, raspberries, blackberries, blueberries, or caramel, pecan, and chocolate. He fills us up with his goodness: hope, peace, love, grace, and mercy.

Faithfulness – Baking, cooking, and creating take time to learn. Faith is nothing without action. It's a process, and we must be faithful to keep showing up to continue to grow and learn in the process.

Gentleness – Be gentle with the crust. It will crumble easily. Be gentle with yourself and others, just like he is.

Self-control – Self-control has to be the hardest thing to learn in baking and cooking. I want to rush in and taste it all, but it's not all for me. It's for sharing with others. Don't overindulge. Gather your friends and savor the pie and your time together.

Today's Slice of the Pie

▲ Take something in your life and apply the fruits of the Spirit to it. Maybe it's your husband? Your art? Your kids? Your work? Yourself?

▲ What fills you up and allows you to pour out? How is God using this thing to show you his love so that you can then share his love with others?

Ann's Pecan Pie

Yield: 1 pie

INGREDIENTS

1 1-pound Royers dough ball
⅓ cup butter, melted
1 cup sugar
1 cup light corn syrup
1 teaspoon vanilla
1 teaspoon salt
4 eggs
1½ cups pecan halves

INSTRUCTIONS

Preheat oven to 350°F.

Roll out the dough ball and place into a 9-inch pie pan to form a pie shell.

Mix the butter, sugar, corn syrup, vanilla, and salt together by hand. Then mix in the eggs.

Pour the filling into the pie shell and cover with pecans. Bake for 45 minutes. The filling should be set and a knife should come out cleanly.

35

Grace Always

If someone is caught in a sin, you who live by the
Spirit should restore that person gently. But watch
yourselves, or you also may be tempted.

GALATIANS 6:1

Last year, I had a tough time with a friend. I thought
maybe I did something to hurt her, but I didn't know
what I may have done. And maybe it wasn't about
me at all. Maybe she was in a rough place and wanted
to be quiet. What I did know was that I wanted to
keep loving her, even if it was something as simple
as a loving comment on Instagram or a text to ask a
question about something she was knowledgeable in.
God continually placed her on my heart, and I would
wonder, *Really? She hasn't reached out to me! Why do*

I have to keep loving? I'm so glad that God has never said that to me!

Satan tries to divide us, but we can't get caught up in his plan to tear us apart from one another. Instead, we need to give grace, encourage our friends, and pray for them. We need to be the light for people fighting hard battles. That same friend eventually sent me a text over a year later, thanking me for being there for her when she wasn't there for me. I was so excited to see our relationship come full circle. We don't have to do much to give grace to others. We honestly have to love like Jesus, and he will do the rest.

Keep loving others and extending grace even when you don't get much in return. God may just be using you to help someone through a difficult time. Then, when you are facing challenges of your own, he will send someone to you to do the same.

Today's Slice of the Pie

▲ Is there someone in your life against whom you sometimes want to put up a wall and forget?

▲ How can you give them grace or let them off the hook?

▲ How can you keep loving them from a distance today?

36

He Restores

He restores my soul. He leads me in paths
of righteousness for his name's sake.

PSALM 23:3 ESV

I've talked about playing the victim card and about
broken relationships. I mentioned that the relationship
between my parents was painful, and our family
business was tearing us apart. Since I was a little girl,
I always dreamed of a daddy-daughter relationship
like in the movies. I wanted to run to my daddy when
I fell and scraped my knee, and I wanted to be able to
call him with good news and have him be my biggest
cheerleader. I wanted his lap to be the safest place to
crawl up into and cry, but we didn't have that kind of

relationship. Our relationship was built around work and our family café. Every conversation was about who came in to eat dinner at the café, whether or not I ordered the food for the weekend, or how much money I needed to put in his checking account. As I stayed in the family business, our relationship only became more difficult, and it was not what I wanted my life or my relationship with him to look like.

Remember how I talked about Brave Girl Camp in Idaho? At camp, I learned that I had a choice, that my dad was not doing anything on purpose to hurt me, and that he was doing the best he could from his past experiences. He couldn't give me what I dreamed of because he didn't know what that looked like. He had never experienced it from his parents. I realized that God was the only Father that I needed to run to. He would give me all the things I hoped for and more. Learning to let my dad off the hook opened up our relationship to healing. I was able to meet him exactly where he was on his walk and love him for who he was: a broken father who was doing the best he could to love a broken daughter. A couple of years ago, he told me that I could share our story of healing and restoration. Now I can share about how I do call him, how we go to the movies together, and how when I tell him all about the exciting things going on in my life, he cheers me on. God can truly restore the most broken of relationships.

he makes all things BEAUTIFUL in his time

TODAY'S SLICE OF THE PIE

▲ What relationships in your life need restoration? Do you believe God can restore them?

▲ What do you need to let go of in order to allow God to heal? Or who do you need to let off the hook?

▲ Who in your life needs to hear that their past does not define who they are in God's eyes?

37

Cry Harder

Blessed are you who hunger now,
for you will be satisfied.
Blessed are you who weep now,
for you will laugh.

LUKE 6:21

Stop me when this starts to sound familiar. *I don't want to cry; I'll mess up my makeup. If I cry, it will look like I am weak. I don't want to cry; I don't have time to deal with that right now.* Does any of that sound familiar? I've always disliked the quote, "Suck it up, buttercup." I believe sucking it up and pushing it down only causes the hurt, pain, anger, and bitterness to deepen. Embrace what's hard. Cry it out and don't hold it in.

Sit in the brokenness, the pain, and the difficult times. Grieve. Grieving is part of the process, and sometimes we don't take the time to do it properly. We continue to push the hurt down deeper and go about life. Then something happens and triggers something stuffed away in us. Someone says something or an experience brings back the painful moment we thought we had moved past. So how do we handle the grief?

Jesus lives inside of us, and he lived through the same sadness we experience. He knew that he was going to be betrayed, nailed to a cross, stabbed in the side. He knew what was coming, and he embraced the grief. He embraces it with us. He is right in the middle and knows what pain you are feeling. He walked among us so he could understand our human nature. He is one with God and is catching all your tears. Won't you sit at his feet and cry out to him. Just try it. Don't just whisper the words. Talk to him with your voice. Let him introduce himself to you again and remind you that you are going to be OK because he IS. And don't forget the helpers he sends alongside us, who give us a shoulder to cry on, who comfort, love, and hold us like Jesus does. Friend, don't hold it in. Whatever you are facing right now, cry out to Jesus.

Today's Slice of the Pie

▲ Are you a big crier, or do you stuff down your feelings?

▲ Was there something someone said to make you think crying was a bad thing? What was it? How was crying looked down upon in your family?

▲ What do you need to cry out to Jesus about today?

38

Get Outta Your Own Way

Let us also lay aside every weight, and sin which clings so closely, and let us run with endurance the race that is set before us, looking to Jesus.

HEBREWS 12:1–2 ESV

I was visiting with a friend recently and she mentioned how many opportunities she had missed out on in her life. Time after time she would tell me how someone had "taken" her idea and done something with it. In her mind, all of her ideas had to be worked out to perfection before she would even start a project or launch an idea. She wouldn't even start because the feeling of finishing "less than" would paralyze her.

I could definitely relate to how she was feeling

because I've struggled with the same thing. I used to get so hung up on trying to make things seem perfect in our home. I couldn't have anything out of place before an event, and the pressure was suffocating. Then, during the event I would be so caught up in the all the details that I would miss out on the community. Perfection is a lie and has been from the minute Adam and Eve ate the apple. Through the years, I've learned that my directions are simple: show up with empty hands and let God lead.

Letting go of control and perfection is still somewhat new to me. I've found that most of the time I just need to stop worrying and quit overthinking. We tend to overthink things in our lives and not follow God's simple prompts that come through a text from a friend, a song, a speed bump, a conversation, a single word that he lays on our hearts. So often, we get in our own way.

My friend and I kept chatting about what it felt like to be stuck, frozen, and without a clue as to how to begin. We realized there are common lies that we tell ourselves that leave us stuck. For me, one of the big fat lies I tell myself often is: *Nobody wants to hear what I have to say*. Wrong! My words are precisely for who God puts in front of me. Maybe you think, *Everyone else is already doing what I want to do, so I need to find something else*, or *They do it better*. Not at all! There is plenty of room at God's table for everybody. You were created on purpose, with a purpose. Friend, you have a gift, and God gave it to you to use. We can't be too scared to do what God has laid on our hearts. Sometimes the bravest thing we can do is just start!

God gave me words from my life experiences—from both the salty and sweet experiences. Together they have baked a beautiful story of grace, hope, and love, and I want to share that story so that others may know him. Sometimes I just have to remind myself to get outta my own way and get started.

Today's Slice of the Pie

▲ What do you need to just start?

▲ How can you get outta your own way today?

▲ What is one small thing you can do today to start?

Hee Haw Pie

Yield: 1 savory pie

INGREDIENTS

1 1-pound herb dough ball
1 red onion, diced
1 tablespoon butter
1 tablespoon chopped garlic
½ pound bacon, cut in pieces
1 cup ground sausage
1 tablespoon jalapeños
1 cup shredded cheddar
4 eggs
¾ cup heavy whipping cream

INSTRUCTIONS

Preheat oven to 350°F.

Roll out the herb dough ball and place into a 9-inch pie pan to form a pie shell.

In a skillet over medium heat, melt the butter. Add the onions and garlic. Sauté until the onions are transparent. Transfer the onions and garlic to a bowl and set aside.

Sauté the bacon and sausage.

Mix all the ingredients.

Fill the herb pie shell with filling. Bake for 35 to 40 minutes.

39

Grace and Mercy

Have mercy on me, O God, according to your unfailing love; according to your great compassion blot out my transgressions. Wash away all my iniquity and cleanse me from my sin.

PSALM 51:1–2

Recently I scheduled three hours of the day to sit and do nothing but write and create. Instead, I chose to clean the house, weed the flower beds, lay in the hammock, shop for groceries, pay some bills, paint my toenails, and do a ton of other things that have zero to do with writing and creating. Yes, all of those things needed to be done, but they were *not* what I needed to be focusing on.

Let's face it: we do not always make the best choices in life. Sometimes I push the snooze button for over an hour, and then I don't get up in time to sit with Jesus before I greet the day and my family. The next thing I know, the entire day gets away from me, and I haven't even made the time to say "Hi" to him. Another bad choice I make repeatedly is to eat sugar! Oh, the sugar. I've tried every diet, magic potion, and fat burning machine out there, and I continually fall short.

I was recently talking with a friend about my fleshy struggle and bad choices with food, and she reminded me that we have to deny our flesh and rely on God completely to fulfill all of our needs. Jesus says, "Whoever wants to be my disciple must deny themselves and take up their cross and follow me" (Matthew 16:24). I have known before that I can easily fall into my own selfish ways. My intention is to do what is right, but sometimes I need a big "aha" moment to cause a shift in my life and change me on the inside.

My friend's words were exactly what I needed to hear: deny your flesh. I'm tired of breaking promises to myself and to God. I'm so grateful for his unfailing grace and mercy over my life. He knows that I'm going to fail and give in to the flesh over and over, but that's where his grace comes in.

Today's Slice of the Pie

- ▲ Where in your life do you continually give in to your selfish desires?

- ▲ What can you do to quit breaking that promise to yourself and God?

- ▲ What would it look like to deny your flesh and follow him in that area?

40

Five Cardinals

"Am I a God who is near," declares the Lord,
"And not a God far off?"

JEREMIAH 23:23 NASB

For the past nine years, we have owned a commercial kitchen called the Bake Shop in a small town about forty-five minutes from our home. It's where we baked most of our family's pies. All the pies we ship to customers across the country came out of that kitchen. When Rick and I bought those seven acres in Brenham, Texas, we built a three-thousand-square-foot building to house a business that God ended up taking us out of. Initially, we were at a loss for what we were supposed to put on the land, and then God hit us over the head and said, *Move the commercial kitchen here.* I was never passionate about driving forty-five minutes to the Bake Shop to create and dream. And even though we were grateful for that season, we were excited about the opportunity to bring our business five minutes from our home.

Moving the kitchen was a much bigger task than we had envisioned. The business God took us out of provided enough money for us to finish out most of the building and move, but we still had five big projects that needed thousands of dollars to complete, and I was overcome with fear and exhaustion. Rock and dirt cost $4,000, AC cost $20,000, a stove cost $5,000, refrigeration cost $13,000, and there was one other major expense, but I don't remember it now. Funny, huh, considering how much I worried about it at the time? Sometimes what we think is so extraordinarily significant in the moment is something we forget quickly afterwards. As Rick was quickly listing off each one of these five things, I could not help but to break down into tears. I wondered, *How the heck are we going to pay for this?* I reached out to my prayer warriors, sisters, and dreamers, asking them to stand in prayer over this piece of holy land. I prayed for provision, peace, comfort, and guidance in making decisions that would give God all of the glory. I prayed to completely trust in him and allow him to take the fear out of the equation, and when I did, I immediately began to calm down.

As Rick and I were leaving the new property, I

looked up and watched five beautiful cardinals fly directly in front of us. Five, not one. One for each of the things we needed. For me, it was a sign that he sees us in the big and the small and that he is faithful and will provide. As soon as I saw the cardinals, I began crying again. But this time they were tears of joy and peace. And, as I tell you all this, all the listed needs were met. The refrigeration. The stove. The rock and dirt. The AC. And that fifth thing that I forgot about.

Today's Slice of the Pie

▲ Has there been a situation where you felt completely overwhelmed, only to have God step in right away and show you it was all going to be okay? What was it?

▲ Has God ever used something to speak to you? Maybe the sky? A rainbow? A song? A bird?

▲ Make a list of the things you need right now. Pray to God, asking him to provide. Then keep that list to see how God has answered prayer over time.

keep
Showing
up

41

Seeing God in Action

A SLICE OF THE PIE FROM MY BROTHER, TODD ROYER

Be still, and know that I am God.

PSALM 46:10

About twenty years ago, my friend and I were having a conversation while stargazing. My friend was more focused on stargazing and saw shooting star after shooting star while I was more caught up in the conversation and kept missing them. I finally focused on looking, but it was too late. Clouds came and blocked our view. I got so wrapped up in the unimportant that I missed out on seeing God in action.

God is moving everywhere, every day, in the big and the small, but if we fill our lives with chatter (electronics, activities, hustle, and bustle), we may miss out on the opportunity to see God's hand at work. "Be still, and know that I am God" requires saying no to the distractions around you and focusing on him. When someone can do that and view the world with that enduring focus, they will see with such clarity. Two things I love to pray for each day are to be a blessing to someone during the day and to see God in action. I need to quit saying I'm going to write down how I've seen God in action and start a journal of my findings. Our minds are simple and we forget, but when we write things down, we can go back and ponder them exactly when our heart, mind, and soul need to be reminded of his work.

Today's Slice of the Pie

▲ What in your life keeps you from seeing God in action?

▲ How can you create space or margin in your life to see God's handiwork?

Stars can't shine without darkness

42

Kind People Are My Kinda People

As God's chosen people, holy and dearly loved, clothe yourselves with compassion, kindness, humility, gentleness, and patience.

COLOSSIANS 3:12

I was walking towards the baseball fields one day with another baseball mom, just making small talk about the lack of sleep and early morning games, when one of the baseball dads walked towards us and hugged the other mom then walked away, not acknowledging me at all. I kept walking and was hurt a bit, but only ten steps later, one of my son's teammates spoke to me from the dugout, "Good morning! How are you?" This sweet boy saw me and had no idea I was disappointed by the lack of compassion from someone else just moments earlier.

It doesn't take much to see people, to see them walking alone or to see sadness in their eyes. How many people do we walk by every day and never look them in the eyes or truly see their faces? It also doesn't take much to speak love and truth over other people. A simple smile. A sincere "How are you?" And what about the people right in front of us—our own family and people we work with every day? Seeing the people we live with day in and day out is not easy. We take them for granted and get into a routine. Those are the ones we so easily forget to see. I continuously have to remind myself to pursue my friends and family, to pour into them and fill them up. When we pour into the people in our lives, they will pour into us. My kids often say, "Don't be a bucket dipper; be a bucket filler!" Let's take it a step further—or maybe a giant leap! How would your day-to-day interactions change if you started to look at everyone through the eyes of Jesus? That's not easy because we don't always see ourselves the way that Jesus does: broken but chosen, made with purpose, loved, seen, heard, and the source of so much joy! He sees the person that hurt my feelings just like he sees me. So today, be kind. Kind people are my kinda people, and I'm guessing they are yours too.

Today's Slice of the Pie

- ▲ Who in your life do you need to stop and see?

- ▲ Do you know what fills their bucket? What can you do today to do that?

- ▲ How do you think Jesus sees you? Do you believe he sees you with hope, love, mercy, kindness, and joy?

Kind People are my kinda People

43

Find Your Tribe

Iron sharpens iron,
and one man sharpens another.

PROVERBS 27:17 ESV

Living in Round Top, Texas, and working in our pie shop and café, we have met many diverse people. On a busy day, over three hundred people walk through our doors. That's three hundred people to connect with and shine on for Jesus. I remember the Saturday Elizabeth and Tomi first walked into the café, dressed for the Junk Gypsy's prom (a big ole get-together to channel your inner prom dress desires). Their hairstyles were the size of Dallas, and their makeup looked like it came straight off the MAC Cosmetics runway. There weren't any available tables at the café, so they took the last two swivel barstools at the counter. I was intrigued by their style and had to ask them where they were going, where they were from, and what they did in the real world. We chatted until they left, hung out later at the prom, and then talked more the next day as they ate their Sunday fried chicken. That was eight years ago, and those girls and I have been there for each other through many trials and celebrations.

LOVE
your
TRIBE

How we met taught me that building a tribe doesn't always look like you might expect. And sometimes what we expect can limit our relationships. So pay attention. You may have to be the one to take the first step. When you go to church or are at work, ask that girl you keep running into if she'd like to join you for lunch. Connect with her and learn from her wisdom and knowledge. There is such beauty in having people in place who are ready at any time to pray for you—people who know your heart and will meet you at anytime and anyplace no matter where you are at that moment. This is your tribe! God is the ultimate relationship conductor and is always bringing people into our lives for different seasons. You are not alone. Your tribe is out there. Now go find 'em.

Today's Slice of the Pie

▲ What fears are keeping you from asking "that girl" at church out for coffee?

▲ Do you ever imagine she might have the same fears too?

▲ Who in your life gets excited about the good happening in your life?

▲ Who do you call when you are struggling and in the dark?

▲ Who can you reach out to this week and ask out for coffee?

Chicken Margherita Pizza Pie

½ yellow onion diced

1 TBSP olive oil
1 TBSP chopped garlic

1 cup fresh mozzarella torn into pieces

½ cup shredded mozzarella

1 cup grated parmesan

½ cup Mayo

1½ cups fresh chicken breast cubed & boiled

3 TBSP fresh chopped basil

2 sliced tomatoes

Preheat oven to 350°
Saute diced onions & garlic in olive oil on medium, until onions are transparent.

In a separate bowl, combine all cheeses, mayonnaise, onions & garlic, chicken & diced basil (leave 1 TBSP out)

Add one layer of tomato slices on bottom of 9" pie crust & layer with cheese, tomatoes & cheese. Sprinkle remaining basil, salt & pepper. Bake for 45 to 60 mins. Lets sit for one hour! ENJOY!

44

It's Never Too Late

A Slice of Pie from My Brother, Micah Royer

Now all glory to God, who is able, through his mighty power at work within us, to accomplish infinitely more than we might ask or think.

Ephesians 3:20 NLT

How often do our perceptions of things or others limit us? It could be a limiting circumstance, such as financial difficulty or a broken or damaged relationship; it could be the way we see a child, a parent, or a spouse; it could be a situation that feels hopeless, such as a dead-end job. We tend to define our reality by how we perceive it to be.

it's never too late as long as you have breath

In the Old Testament, the Lord told Jacob he would be a great leader of the nations, and he was well on his way, with many sons. But of all his sons, Joseph was his beloved (Genesis 37:3). Jacob had a special place in his heart for Joseph, and I can only imagine Jacob's utter devastation when his other sons came home and told him Joseph had been killed.

Little did he know how God was at work. During that entire time, Jacob believed his beloved son was gone. The opportunity to watch his son grow, to converse with him, to share life experiences, and to watch him mature and have a family of his own, all of it was gone, and Jacob believed he had been robbed of every one of those precious opportunities.

Ultimately, however, God turned Jacob's reality on its head when he found out that Joseph was still alive. That moment of embracing one another for the first time after so many years must have been quite poignant. In Genesis 48, we're told how Jacob had the opportunity to bless Joseph's sons, and one can only imagine how blessed Jacob felt to not only have his son back but to be able to bless his grandsons. Sometimes what we think is a lost cause or a hopeless situation God can turn into good and bless far beyond our wildest imagination.

Today's Slice of the Pie

▲ What issues have you given up on because it feels hopeless and lost?

▲ What areas of your life are you limiting God's power?

▲ How can you open up your heart to the idea that God's desire to bless you is more significant than you could ever hope for or anticipate?

45

Taste and see

Taste and see that the Lord is good;
blessed is the one who takes refuge in him.

PSALM 34:8

My dad always says, "A customer eats the food with
their eyes first!" When you walk into our family café,
what you get is sensory overload. You cannot step
into the café and not see the fifteen-foot bar lined
with thirty whole, handmade pies, and the walls
and ceiling covered with treasures, old menus, and
memorabilia. As you're seated, you're given a menu
with so many choices while warm, homemade rolls
with herb and applesauce butters are placed in front
of you. You finally order, and then you patiently wait

taste and see that He is good.

for the waitress to deliver your food. You are expecting nothing but the best. Your plate comes out, and your eyes grow like a child on Christmas morning. The pork tenderloin dressed with a peach and pepper glaze covers the platter while the scoops of mashed potatoes and creamed corn are heaped up next to it. It's better than you could have ever imagined. Oh, then there's the pie. The pie is warm, and the ice cream is melting on top of it. When you are finished eating, you push away from the table in sheer delight and look forward to telling the next person you see to come and be served here.

Isn't this just like God? He puts something good in front of us, we taste it, and we know that he is the best chef ever. He is faithful and continues to serve us well. Because we have seen the work he's done in our lives, we begin to expect and have faith in him to do great things. He is steadfast and continues to pour out and give abundantly. We eat of his goodness, and our hearts, mind, and souls are full. We are so excited about what we have tasted and can't wait to go and share it with the world.

Today's Slice of the Pie

▲ Can you recall a recent meal that left you feeling completely satisfied and you could not wait to tell the next person you saw about it? What was it?

▲ Now, can you recall a time that God left you completely stuffed and satisfied?

▲ Did you run and tell someone? Share with a friend this week the story of how you tasted and saw God's goodness!

46

I've Got 99 Problems

A Slice of Pie from My Mom, Dr. Karen Royer

He replied, "Because you have so little faith.
Truly I tell you, if you have faith as small as a mustard
seed, you can say to this mountain,
'Move from here to there,' and it will move.
Nothing will be impossible for you."

MATTHEW 17:20

For many years now, I have had the privilege of
working with folks who have seemingly impossible,
mountainous obstacles in their lives. To them, I often
say, "The answer is always Jesus; we just need to
trust him." I believe this to be a true but not simple

answer. I, too, have struggled with those mountains at times in my life. When Brayden, Tara's oldest, was about two or three years old, he said to me, "Gommy, what do you do for work?" I answered, "I help people with their problems." He immediately exclaimed: "Pwoblems, pwoblems, I got lotsa pwoblems!"

Do you have "lotsa pwoblems" in your life? Of course you do! However, Jesus only requires faith as small as a mustard seed for us to move mountains! Have you ever seen a mustard seed? They are incredibly small, not much bigger than the period at the end of this sentence. But that's all the faith we need. God has all the answers to our biggest questions. He will rush to meet you. He cannot wait to hold you with his strong arms! He wants to be with you! You only need to ask.

Today's Slice of the Pie

▲ Where is your faith too small for a problem?

▲ What is keeping you from trusting in God for the answer?

▲ What can you turn over to him right now?

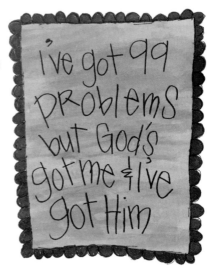
i've got 99 PRobleMS but God's got me & i've got Him

47

The Beginning, Middle, and End

Know therefore today, and take it to your heart,
that the Lord, He is God in heaven above
and on the earth below; there is no other.

DEUTERONOMY 4:38 NASB

I have wanted to share this story for so long. It's one
of my favorites. Rick and I had been dating for a short
time, maybe a month, when he offered to help cater
an event. This was the first time he had helped out at a
catering, or any business function for that matter. It had
always been a dream of his to be in family business.

(Crazy, right?) Well, it was a beautiful Saturday morning—the perfect day to cater a wedding in the country. We loaded up the vehicles with all the china, equipment, and fantastic food and headed out. My mom and I were in Rick's truck while my dad and Rick were in another vehicle. We pulled up to the venue to unload, and I jumped out and locked the truck. With the keys inside. Yep, I locked the truck with the keys inside along with all the cold items needed for the wedding. Of course, I was frantic! I didn't want to ruin someone's wedding or have to ask Rick to break his window. I mean, we'd just met! Everyone went to set up the venue with the food and equipment that wasn't inside the truck, and I stood between the car and the chapel, watching for the bride and groom to come out. Rick had stuff in the truck to break in, but that obviously wasn't helping. And we were in the middle of nowhere, so it's not like the cops could be there quickly.

Finally, after about an hour, an officer showed up to help. He worked on getting in the truck for about twenty minutes with no success. My dad kept saying, "Break the window!" I could sense Rick's concern. And there I was, smack dab in the middle of ruining a wedding, breaking my boyfriend's window, and having my dad frustrated with me. My mind was swirling. Rick asked the officer if he could give it a go. I begged for mercy. I prayed, *Lord, please unlock this truck!* About that time, the guests started coming out of the church, and Rick said, "Let me try one more time, and if I don't get in, I'll break the window." And he got it! Praise the

Lord! I remember Rick telling me after the fact that he was pleading with the Lord also and was just about to give up. We grabbed everything from inside the truck and ran it like mad into the venue. Nobody from the wedding knew a thing! We learned that under pressure, in the middle and the hard, we can continue to walk with God, lean into him, and know that he will make a way. We might not know what the end will look like, but we can be sure that he will always be present. Everyone lived a little happier that day, and we learned a few lessons for the next beginning.

Today's Slice of the Pie

▲ Reflect on a time when you were stuck in the middle and begging for mercy. How did you feel?

▲ How did God show up for you?

▲ Take a moment and give him thanks for his continued presence through the beginning, middle, and end.

Blueberry Lemon Pie

Yield: 1 9-inch pie

INGREDIENTS

1 1-pound Royers dough ball

BLUEBERRY FILLING

4 cups frozen blueberries
1¼ cups sugar
¼ cup lemon juice
½ cup flour
1 cup water

LEMON CREAM CHEESE FILLING

½ pound cream cheese
½ cup powdered sugar
1 teaspoon vanilla
1 tablespoon lemon juice
1 egg
½ cup flour
1 teaspoon lemon zest

CRUMBLE PIE TOPPING

1 cup brown sugar • ¾ teaspoons cinnamon
¼ pound butter • 1 cup oatmeal
½ cup flour • ⅛ teaspoon salt
Pinch of nutmeg

Instructions

Preheat oven to 300°F.

Roll out the dough ball and place into a 9-inch pie pan to form a pie shell.

For the blueberry filling, mix the blueberries, sugar, and lemon juice in a braising pot and bring to a boil. Meanwhile, mix the flour and water together. When the blueberry filling mixture comes to a boil, add the flour and water mixture to it, whipping constantly to even thickness.

For the lemon cream cheese filling, add all ingredients together in a bowl and mix until smooth.

For the crumble topping, add the dry ingredients together in a bowl and mix. Add the melted butter and mix, making sure there are no dry spots.

Next, spread half of the blueberry filling (approximately 1½ cups) in the bottom of the pie shell. Using a spatula, layer ¼ inch of the lemon cream cheese filling (approximately ¾ cup). Then, spread the second half of the blueberry filling over the lemon cream cheese layer. Lightly top with the crumble topping (approximately 3 tablespoons), spreading it evenly over the pie.

Bake at 300°F for 30 to 40 minutes until golden brown and crunchy.

48

The Word Just

You can't pick and choose in these things,
specializing in keeping one or two things
in God's law and ignoring others.

JAMES 2:10 MSG

If it was me and I saw the title of this devotional, I don't know that I would think of the word *just* as being a "bad" word. But for me, using the word *just* limits my mind and keeps me comfortable or in a constant state of temptation or addiction. *Oh, it's just one margarita. Oh, I'm just a mom. It's just one scoop of ice cream.* Or, *It's just one pair of shoes.* I catch myself saying it often, and when I reflect on the conversation or thought, most often it's a lie.

Today I found myself saying, "Oh, I'm just finishing

up a piece of art." No! A piece of art is not *just* a thing. It's something that I was created to do by the Father. It's a gift that has been given to me to share about him. For you, creating art might be an outlet to channel your pain or anger or a form of therapy. There is nothing "just" about that.

My boys use this word all the time when they are wrapped up in a video game. When I ask them to stop the game, the usual response is, "Just a few more minutes, please?" That becomes a few more minutes, and then they cross the line into disrespect.

Lies are the enemy's ways of keeping us living in temptation, addiction, or disrespect at all times, and he can trap us with something as simple as a word. We have to choose the truth over lies. We have to choose "just" Jesus.

Today's Slice of the Pie

▲ Is there a word like *just* that you use daily that limits you?

▲ What areas of your life do you not "just" choose Jesus?

▲ Reflect and ask him to "just" be your everything.

49

Room at the Table for All

> After he said this, he took some bread
> and gave thanks to God in front of them all.
> Then he broke it and began to eat.
>
> Acts 27:35

It took me many years to grasp the spiritual significance of what the table is all about, which is so much more than food and service. Don't get me wrong. The food and service need to be good, but the table is all about making and building relationship as *them all* share a meal together.

At the café there are only eleven tables, and we share tables. We can't guarantee a table, but we can

174

guarantee a seat. Often, *them all* are seated at a table and have no idea who is sitting at the other end of the table. Sitting with strangers can be awkward at first, but if you open yourself up to being real and vulnerable, it can turn into a delightful and memorable experience—an experience that will open up the opportunity for further community and relationship in his kingdom. I've been asked by guests numerous times if the folks they shared a table with the last time happened to be dining. I loved hearing the story a customer shared once of how the folks they sat with one time ended up inviting them to their daughter's wedding.

These "shared table" relationships are impactful on *them all,* and the table is what makes it all happen. Thus, I've come to realize the table is a very sacred setting, an altar for strangers, friends, and family to gather around to honor him.

Today's Slice of the Pie

▲ Who have you shared a table with recently?

▲ In what ways do those experiences enrich your life and give you a sense of community?

▲ Are there people you don't know well that you can invite to your table?

there's enough room at the table for EVERYONE; you just have to show up and be ready for the best FEAST he has for you.

50

Faith over Fear

Be strong and courageous. Do not be afraid or terrified because of them, for the Lord your God goes with you; he will never leave you nor forsake you.

DEUTERONOMY 31:6

In 1987, my parents loaded up a car that someone had given to us and moved me and my three younger brothers to the small town—eighty-seven people small to be exact—of Round Top, Texas. We were going to take over the Round Top Café, a hole in the wall joint that had two pie flavors, apple and buttermilk. We showed up with nothing but our belongings; our hands were empty. This wasn't a dream of ours. It was a gift. At the time we knew it was an opportunity to start over and make a fresh beginning. My dad had been out of work for nearly four years, and finding a job in the restaurant industry was hard after the oil bust in Houston. But the owners of the Round Top Café knew my parents and that our family needed work, so they gave my dad $200 in the cash drawer and told him they would work on a payment plan once we got settled. My parents took a massive leap of faith and had no idea how things would work out, but their faith was greater than their fear.

We didn't pick pie; it chose us. I guess you could say the crust was a strong foundation. When we took this little country café over, we knew nothing about cooking, running a restaurant business, or pie. What my dad did know was how to market a good slice of pie, make someone feel seen when they walked through the door, and tell them what they wanted to eat. Most people were escaping reality when they came to visit Round Top, and they didn't want to have to make a decision. They wanted to show up and be loved and lavished on. My dad also knew that God was in control, and he was the only one who could orchestrate this move to Round Top. Looking back on the history of the café, I can see all the times that faith carried us through the tough seasons. Yes. A good pie crust and a whole lot of faith.

TODAY'S SLICE OF PIE

▲ Can you think of a time in your life when you let fear overtake your faith? What was the outcome?

▲ Is there something in your life that you are living in fear about?

▲ Give that fear over to the Lord and ask him to show you how to walk in faith.

faith over fear

51

Blessed Are the Peacemakers

A Slice of the Pie from My Brother, J. B. Royer

Blessed are the peacemakers:
for they shall be called children of God.

Matthew 5:9 KJV

When my sister asked me to help write a devotional, I was honored, yet I kept putting it off in hopes that something would come to mind. I started thinking about what some of my strengths are, and my wife said, "You're great at keeping peace." I'm certainly not perfect at this, but I do value keeping peace with others. As you walk through life, there are many struggles, anxieties, and hard times, and I've learned that maintaining peace in all situations will give you true peace.

Now, don't mistake peacekeeping for peacemaking! Go back and read day five if you need a refresher on the difference between these concepts. Peacekeeping will not give you the peace that you are looking for. Why? Because peacekeeping allows you to make an easy choice in the moment, but it often means you must sacrifice your morals. Then, in the long term, the road only gets bumpier. Peacemakers will do the opposite. They will choose to speak truth even when it's hard, but they'll do so with grace and mercy.

Go out today and make peace with someone without forsaking your values.

Today's Slice of the Pie

- ▲ When have you failed at making peace or sacrificed your values to keep momentary peace?

- ▲ Who do you need to make peace with in your life?

- ▲ Can you speak the truth with grace and mercy? What should that look like?

Hot Chocolate Pie

Preheat oven 350°
9" unbaked pie crust

combine together
½ cup softened

Butter

1½ cups white sugar

2 eggs

2 tsps Vanilla
beat 'til creamy

POUR in
2 cups of flour

⅓ cup of cocoa powder
⅓ tsp baking soda
½ cup peppermint baking chips
Mix 'til smooth

Scoop into piecrust, press filling down, bake 50 mins.

take pie out of oven & turn to low broil. sprinkle top of pie with 1 cup of small marshmallows
+ place in oven for 2 to 5 mins. nice & toasty!
DON'T WALK AWAY

Heat in microwave for one minute

1 cup caramel bits

1 cup chocolate chips

Stir 'til melted & drizzle over marshmallows.

(or use caramel & chocolate sauce)

52

A Medal for You

May the God of peace who brought again from the dead our Lord Jesus, the great shepherd of the sheep, by the blood of the eternal covenant, equip you with everything good that you may do his will, working in us that which is pleasing in his sight, through Jesus Christ, to whom be glory forever and ever. Amen.

HEBREWS 13:20-21 ESV

We don't have to do anything to earn our Father's love. We only need to believe that the only way to him is through his son, Jesus, trusting that Jesus died for all our sins and that we are covered with his grace, love, and mercy. Jesus knows how hard life is because he dwelt among us before he died for our sins. He knew that he had to die to take on our sin and cover us with his grace. I can imagine God smiling down on us when we look up from our mistakes and ask for forgiveness. I see God crying when we suffer because of someone else's sin. I envision God's arms wide open when things of this world crush us. You don't need to perform; he is well pleased with you.

Friend, don't give up. You have come so far, and he hasn't left you yet. Keep showing up and honoring the roads you have traveled and the roads still ahead of you. Remember, you have done hard things and will be OK in the end. Life will continue to be challenging at times, and I know that you have everything inside of you to keep fighting the battles in front of you. I am so proud of you and honored to stand with you. I want to give you a medal as a reminder that we are in this together, and I never want you to forget how far you have come. My hope and prayer for you is to see this medal as a reminder that you are capable, you are equipped, and the living God who endured nails lives inside of you! Don't forget that you were made for this job, and you are the right girl.

Today's Slice of the Pie

▲ Do you feel like a warrior? Write down the things that you have done that make you a warrior!

▲ Do you see how far you have come? And look, you're still standing! Share how you are a victor in your story and how God has equipped you to keep showing up.

▲ Write a letter to your younger self sharing what she will go through and telling her that she will come out on the other side victorious and ready to shout her story from anywhere God sends her.

He is well pleased

Salted Turtle Pecan Pie

FIRST

Preheat oven to 350°
Start with a 9" pie crust, roll out & place in pie pan.

→ 1 cup of milk chocolate chips
½ cup of heavy whipping cream
melt in microwave for 30 seconds & stir 'til smooth
Spread over pie crust & set aside.

next

combine
⅓ cup melted butter
1 cup of sugar
1 TBSP of vanilla
1 tsp of salt
1 cup of light Karo syrup
4 eggs
whisk ingredients 'til smooth & pour over chocolate

Sprinkle with 1½ cups of pecan halves
Bake for 55 mins or 'til filling is set
Let cool.

finally

heat ½ cup of caramel bits with ¼ cup of heavy whipping cream in the microwave for 30 secs. stir 'til smooth. drizzle on top of pecan pie & sprinkle with sea salt.
Let cool, slice, top with ice cream. EAT.

186

Acknowledgments

Oh God, I have seen you make dreams that I have had in my heart for years come true. You never gave up on me when I ran as far as I could. You picked me and would not let go. You have been the one to orchestrate meetings with those in the writing world exactly when I thought I wasn't the girl for this job. Thank you for picking me! I love being your girl.

This being my first book-writing rodeo, I needed all the help I could get! God knew exactly what he was doing when he sent the wonderful team at Broadstreet Publishing. Bill Watkins, my editor, has been such an amazing teacher and has been so patient with me. Thank y'all for all the hard work on my behalf. Working with y'all has felt like home! Let's celebrate and eat pie!

To Melanie Shankle, I had always admired you from a distance, and one spring day God placed us in the same pasture in Round Top, Texas. And, of course, there was pie. You saw in me what I didn't see in myself. Thank you for following the Holy Spirit's prompting and reaching out to your agent, Lisa Jackson. I adore you!

To my agent, Lisa Jackson, you believed in me from the beginning and didn't push too hard until you knew the time was right. You waited patiently and fought hard for me. You are one of my favorite cheerleaders.

To Kathleen Turner and Paula Fulford, y'all were the two that for years never stopped saying, "You should write a book." Then y'all said, "You will write a book." Now y'all say, "Let's write another book and eat pie." Y'all never stopped speaking truth over my life. Y'all never left through the good and the bad. I love y'all.

My husband, Rick, you have been my biggest cheerleader. You support my crazy God-given visions and usually have to reel me in a bit and help to start making them reality. You have been by my side through so many hills and valleys, and the pie that we slice has been so fulfilling. It tastes like heaven.

My sweet boys, Brayden and Bentley, you have rallied me through this whole process, offered to be my illustrators, and helped push *send*! You are truly a gift, and I'm so grateful I get to be your mama.

To my family, y'all are all part of the story—all the

love, grace, ups and downs, healing, and restoration! Mom, Dad, Micah, JB, Todd, Jamie-Len, Liz, Ashley, Grant, Madie, Tristan, Sadie, Wren, Anne, Steven, and Kathryn, I love y'all.

To all the brave girls I've met because of Brave Girls Club, you know who you are. Melody Ross, thank you for pouring your life out and creating a curriculum to share with the rest of us. It truly was the pivot in my life that freed me from the bondage of lies, shame, guilt, and blame.

My Wednesday night Bible study gals, y'all are my favs to have around the table.

And, my grace gang, Abbie and Clarissa, y'all kept me on task. You know me well and knew exactly what I needed to keep going. Y'all edited and formatted 'til your fingers hurt. And to the rest of the grace gang: Alisha, Kristi, Sooze, Danna, Jenn, Elizabeth, Tomi, Brandy, Kellie, Sarah, Merritt, Bobby and Danielle, Tammy, Terra, Debbie, Jolie, Jeane, Tiffany, Haley, Joan, Misti, Heidi, Missy, and Cheryl. Y'all are the best cheerleaders ever!

About the Author

Tara Royer Steele lives in Brenham, Texas, with her husband, Rick, and two boys. She and Rick love being able to work alongside each other. They were called to do life together. She loves to wake up before everyone in the house, put in her AirPods, listen to Bethel Music

Essentials, drink her morning coffee, and let God pour into her heart, mind, and soul. It is where she is filled up, and the Lord gives her a good word to paint and share with the world or tuck away in her heart to ponder.

At the age of twelve, she began working in her family's business, Royers Round Top Café, and continued for thirty-two years. God brought her family to a little town and a small café to take over a place that sold two pies. Those pies grew into something bigger than a café; they grew into a legacy about Jesus through pie. She and her husband own Royers Pie Haven in Round Top, Texas, a place to gather, be encouraged, inspired, loved, and, of course, eat pie. They also have All Things Acres in Brenham, Texas. It is the perfect seven acres that God is using to build something beautiful. For now, they bake the family business's pies there and hold events, retreats, and workshops. Together, they love to create safe spaces for people to gather around the table to create art, bake, eat, and enjoy fellowship. For more information, visit graceupongracegirl.com.